INTERPRETING THE BIBLE

INTERPRETING
THE BIBLE

By
Luke H. Grollenberg

Translated by
Jeanne C. Schoffelen Nooijne
and
Richard Rutherford, C.S.C.

PAULIST PRESS DEUS BOOKS
NEW YORK   GLEN ROCK   WESTMINSTER
TORONTO   AMSTERDAM

A Deus Books Edition of Paulist Press, originally published under the title *Inleiding tot de bijbel* by N. V. Uitgeversmaatschappij Elsevier, Netherlands, © 1966.

NIHIL OBSTAT:
Robert E. Hunt, S.T.D.
Censor Librorum

IMPRIMATUR:
✠ Thomas A. Boland, S.T.D.
Archbishop of Newark

January 18, 1968

Library of Congress
Catalog Card Number: 68-20849

Published by Paulist Press
Editorial Office: 304 W. 58th St., N.Y., N.Y. 10019
Business Office: Glen Rock, New Jersey 07452

Printed and bound in the
United States of America

CONTENTS

FOREWORD   1

    I   The Bible for Every Man?   3
   II   The Living God   12
  III   God Chooses Mankind   22
  IV   God's Wrath and Mercy   33
   V   The Problem of Evil   43
  VI   Warnings and Threats   53
 VII   The Message of Jesus   64
VIII   How the Gospels Were Written   74
  IX   Understanding the Gospels   86
   X   The Words of Jesus   98
  XI   The Paradise Story   114
 XII   Truth and Fiction   126

FOREWORD

This book is the product of twelve discussions on the bible which were presented in the fall and early winter of 1965 on the Dutch television network. They're being reprinted here at the suggestion of a number of viewers who saw the programs in The Netherlands.

Naturally a few things had to be changed in transcribing the material from video-tape into written form. However, in most cases the more-or-less disorganized nature of each discussion was preserved. It may seem even more disorderly in print, because the questions and remarks of several persons taking part in the discussions are italicized without distinction.

The author wishes to express his gratitude to Mrs. Jeanne C. Schoffelen Nooijen, M.A., for her interest in this project and her initial translation of this book. He is also indebted to Richard Rutherford, C.S.C., for his revision and final editing of the English translation.

L. G.

ONE:
The Bible for Every Man?

In the course of these twelve discussions, we shall be concerned with people who put the bible together. The "complete library in one volume," which the bible is, didn't just happen. It came into being through a process that took centuries in growing.

We must choose where to start. We shall begin with the old stories of Samson and David. Then we shall ask why were they told, passed on, and written in that form. For this reason we shall begin with the motivation of the biblical narrators and authors.

Perhaps in that way we may find the answer to the question of why Christianity has come to honor this intricate book with its enormous variety of human expressions as "the book par excellence" (this is the meaning of the word *bible*) and even as "God's word." Perhaps we may, for an approach via the road of history demands considerable attention and perseverance.

A Library in One Volume

According to statistics the bible is the most widely distrib-uted book ever produced. But is it also the most widely read book? Many Christians doubt it. Especially after buying a bible from a door-to-door salesman, a family may ask: "What are we supposed to do with it?" They can't find their way around in it.

Is this the reason why you put a question mark behind the title of this chapter?

Yes, and a big one at that. In our future discussions we shall see that the bible as it is can hardly be a book for everybody, because it is really a whole library in one volume. It contains episodes from widely different times, written by all kinds of persons. And it still holds true that you can only understand an ancient piece of literature well if you know a little bit about the man who wrote it, what urged him to write, what he intended to say, and so on. In writing the bible hundreds of people, if not more, were involved.

I sometimes make the following comparison. Imagine that there is a world library somewhere. All the literature that was ever published has been collected there. During a bombing attack a direct hit ruins and burns the whole place. The librarians go about in the shambles and gather remnants, pieces of manuscripts and legible pages from books and tie them all together. They sort them to some extent, arranging them more according to size rather than by chronological order. A recent page from a newspaper may follow a decree of parliament from the seventeenth century, after which perhaps a few paragraphs of civil law. A poem by a modern author precedes a medieval ballad. In the section on history you see a few old regional legends which were recorded and edited in 1860, followed by a number of pages from a modern history book.

This comparison is not very realistic, but it serves to explain the wide variety in the contents of the bible. Although the bible was never hit by a bomb, it grew during a long historical process which took centuries. In the course of this time a whole lot of literature was lost, and the saved pieces were gradually put together. Once we realize we must know the background of an old piece of writing to be able to appreciate it, we shall also realize that it takes a great deal of background information to understand the bible.

You make the bible sound like nothing more than a textbook. Yet it seems to me that the Church Fathers such as St. Augustine got their inspiration merely by opening the bible at random and meditating on any passage that happened to appear.

True, but I wonder if modern man should still do likewise. Apparently there are still people who live by the bible and use it in this manner. If one happens to be in trouble he opens the bible at random, and the text which comes to his attention first is considered to be God's message to him at that particular moment. Such use of the bible is for many people a part of their religious life. This method was handed down to them by many generations who did the same. For this reason their good faith should be respected. But we have the right to doubt if the average educated modern man would not prefer to ask for the background and the original meaning of a text which he comes across in the bible.

If I understand you correctly, you advocate the historical approach to the bible. In reading it, should we start at the beginning or somewhere else?

Wait a minute. First I'd like to acquaint you a little with the historical approach, and I want to do this with a few stories. Most Catholics still know some fragments of bible stories they learned at school. It seems to me a good idea to look at

a number of these as they occur in the bible. I want to begin
with Samson.

How the Samson Story Grew

This story is to be found in chapters thirteen through six-
teen in the book of Judges. I can best explain part of the historical background by referring you to a map of Palestine, a
small country with very simple geographical boundaries.
About the year 1200 B.C. the Israelite tribes were living in
the inland mountains which form the backbone of the
country. At that time the Philistines established themselves in
the plain along the sea in the Southwest. They came from
Asia Minor or Crete. Soon they began to fight with the Israelites for possession of the fertile rolling country between the
coastal plain and the central mountains. This tense situation
lasted longer than a half a century. At times there were skir-
mishes, more often individual actions by farmers. Such a period of battle and warfare is the very time to circulate stories
of heroic deeds and to exaggerate them.

Perhaps you remember this, at least the older ones among
you, from those days in May 1940 when the Germans overran
the Netherlands and other European countries. I remember
very well that we in Nijmegen heard stories about brave
Dutch soldiers. For instance, there was a story of a soldier at
one end of the great dam separating the North Sea from a
large inland lake, who waited each time until the whole dam
was filled with Germans, and then he shot all of them into
the sea with one lengthwise shot. Then the dam filled up with
a new wave of Germans which he again shot into the sea.
And I believed the story and repeated it. Here's another story:
a man was duck hunting on a big lake in the neighborhood

of Amsterdam on the morning of the German attack. Instead of ducks he saw German fighter planes, Messerschmidts, pass low across the lake heading for the big airport of Schiphol. He shot them down one after the other, dozens of them.

This was the kind of story that we believed and passed on to others because it boosted our patriotic spirit, as you can well understand.

But they could have been pure lies or a lot of bragging!

No, they weren't lies, because our soldiers did fight courageously. The word bragging is not at all fitting here, for bragging is done by someone who wants to draw attention to himself. We told each other such stories to lift our courage and our morale.

During the years of occupation that followed, something else happened that can throw some light on the Samson stories. Many brave acts performed by a number of men in the resistance movement gradually centered around one member of the group. Perhaps you can imagine how it happened: John sabotaged the enemy, Peter played the Germans a dirty trick, but it was Hubert, one of the leaders in the movement, who finally became the big hero. Eventually all these acts of resistance were attributed to him.

This very same thing happened in ancient Israel. Perhaps you know that in an old record of David's companions and of their heroic deeds (Sam. 2, 21), the slaying of Goliath is attributed to a certain Elkanan from Bethlehem. So we may certainly take it for granted that something similar could have happened in the case of Samson.

Furthermore, as the stories about Samson developed, we come across a particular phenomenon with which we in this modern western world are not familiar. In telling stories the Israelites loved to use enigmas and figures of speech; they also loved a play on words to explain the meaning of proper names. For instance, do you know what the name Baton Rouge means? An Israelite would explain the name with a story such as this: In 1699, when Iberville, a French nobleman, was on an expedition to make the first voyage up the Mississippi River from the Gulf of Mexico, his men made camp at Bayou Manchac. The next day, March 17, 1699 Iberville's party reached the first highlands. There they saw a red pole on the banks of a creek. It was about thirty feet high and bore the heads of a number of bears and fish, all of which looked much like a sacrifice. The Indian guides called the spot Istrouma, which means red pole; the French then named it in their language, Baton Rouge.

In the same manner the Israelites found it fascinating and instructive to explain all kinds of names. There was a hill called Lehi in the area where the Philistines and the Israelites were constantly fighting. Lehi means "jaw bone." In addition, the word hill is pronounced the same way as the word for "to throw away" in Hebrew. Now you may understand the background of a detail occurring in the story of Samson (Jg. 15, 9-17).

There are many other details, which mean something only to the one who reads the text in Hebrew. Some of these clearly are intended to make the reader and the listener laugh at the ignorant Philistine, allowing them to enjoy a play on words and the ambiguity of words. I have the highest admiration for the bible translator who succeeds in transferring all these intentions of one author into another language.

The Samson stories were apparently not put together in their present sequence until the war with the Philistines belonged to the distant past. Quickly the hero became a so-called Nazarite, a person dedicated to God who had to let his hair grow and who was not allowed to drink wine. Perhaps it was because of this role that the story of a predicted birth was attributed to him.

Why Was This Story Put in the Bible?

Whatever the reason may have been, we miss out on the real and final purpose of the Samson story if we don't read a few other texts of the book of Judges, especially chapters two (11-16) and ten (6-16). Each of these texts also has a particular historical background. We are going to give a very short summary of Israel's history so you may understand the background of those texts. In the beginning Israel is united. After the reign of David and Solomon the kingdom is split into two countries: the northern and larger one—the area of ten tribes which continued to use the old and revered name "Israel"— and the southern kingdom called "Judah," with Jerusalem as its capital. In the ninth century pressure was exerted from the north by the powerful country of Assyria which finally conquered Israel and destroyed its leading class by deportation. Only Judah remained, a small country whose capital was less than seven miles from the Assyrian border.

During those terrifying years following 700 B.C. when Judah narrowly escaped complete annihilation by Assyria, the leaders urged the people in and around Jerusalem to repent before Yahweh. Recalling the old stories when Israel brought forth heroes, they spoke more or less as follows: "Listen well. We are now in a time of need. But this much we know: if enemies threaten and oppress us, which is happening at this moment, and if we call on God with heart and soul, he will send us a savior. I remind you of the stories of the early times, which tell us this. Everytime troubled Israel turned to Yahweh he sent a redeemer. So do the same: Repent, go back to Yahweh and be faithful to him, and he will help you again, for our God is a God saving us from distress."

It was in keeping with such exhortations and admonitions that a number of ancient stories about the judges, passed on by word of mouth, were put into a larger unit. The Samson sequence happens to be one of those stories. The meaning of this unit was explained in the verses from Judges, chapters, two and ten, as we pointed out.

You keep stressing the historical aspects of the bible. I don't know where it's all going. I thought we were supposed to learn of the bible as the source of our spiritual life.

Yes, that is my goal, and this fits in perfectly with your first statement. I believe that the message will be delivered to us precisely by the historical approach. This I hope to unfold little by little. Maybe you are beginning to see it already. When we look at stories like the one of Samson no longer as wondrous tales that we have to believe word for word, but as expressions of conviction, as a certain way of life, then we realize that these stories are an intrinsic part of our own present situation as Christians. They tell us: "God is like this: if you are in need and you call on him, he will help you."

David and Uriah, a Different Kind of Story

For our next discussion I should like to suggest that you read something else besides those few chapters about Samson. You know the story of David who took Bathsheba as his wife and who managed to have her lawful husband killed in action. You will find it a little further on in the bible, in the second book of Samuel, chapters eleven and twelve. Here we have a totally different situation. David lived about 1000 years before Christ, and those chapters eleven and twelve are part of what one might call a kind of biography of David. They are written by a person who was nearby when all the events took place, whereas with Samson there is great time lapse between the endless battles with the Philistines and the final version in which these stories appear in the book of Judges. In David's case we are dealing with a single author, one who was well known at court and who during Solomon's reign wrote about events that had happened recently.

Compare the chapters about Samson with the story of David and Uriah. You will see the great differences between them. With David there are no apparitions of God, no exaggerated heroic feats, no popular humor or tragedy. We have merely the description of what is going on in the hearts and minds of a few people, or, perhaps better, a sober and very precise account of what they do and say.

While you read it take into consideration that this great piece of literature dates from 950 B.C., even before the time of the great Greek poet Homer. He lived in the eighth century or thereabouts; the precise dates are not known. Much later in the fifth century come the great tragedy writers, Aeschylus and Sophocles. Neither the Mesopotamians nor the Egyptians created anything at that time which can compare with the chapters about David. Why then did Israel have such an exceptional gift, and why did it have such an interest in mankind?

TWO:
The Living God

The story of Samson would fill less than a page in a newspaper. Yet these four bible chapters present enough material for a spectacular film, and too much for one discussion. The slaughters at which this God-sent man excelled, and his personal life—which was certainly not chaste—will definitely be among the topics we'll talk about. The story of David and Bathsheba generates all sorts of questions. Whatever possessed this people to relate with such beauty a thoroughly wicked act of its greatest king, and even to include it in its holy book?

I think you're still putting too much stress on historical backgrounds. It's all very interesting, but as a Christian I want to know how I can profit from these stories.

Well, you decided to listen to me and not to somebody else. And in the course of several years I've become convinced that only by probing the historical background and the motivation of the biblical authors can we learn to understand better what they have to say to us Christians. So for the time being you will have to put up with historical information and later you will notice that it is essential. The wondrous and peculiar thing about the bible is that it deals with the true God, who in turn deals with real people. Real people live in history as flesh and blood. No ideas are offered; no concepts, no sublime doctrines are proclaimed. Instead, life is presented as it is.

Don't we confuse the issue by talking about authors? I mean, here we have a Jewish history in which a Jewish author invents a story about a man named Samson who was sent by Yahweh. A Greek writer can interpret his history the same way—with Zeus and so on. And a Roman has even more excuse, because Roman history is filled with so many triumphs.

Let me say that the people of Israel distinguish themselves through their belief in one God. This makes them different from all other nations. Their entire existence is dependent upon that one God. So they interpret everything that happens to them as a function of and in the light of their bond with that one God. This is what makes it so important for us. We have the same convictions; we too recognize one living God who is interested in each of us. So what is being told about the relationship of this God and these people refers also to our relationship with this God.

That's true. I was struck by your phrase "the living God." I just finished reading a few Greek stories, and I noticed that Zeus never has final control over events. Some kind of fate always takes over.

The expression "the living God" is typical of the bible and has quite a number of aspects. Let me mention two of them. All other gods—all gods of the other people in the neighboring areas—are associated with nature, which is subject to the rhythm of winter and summer, of death and revival. The Israelites called Yahweh *the living* God because he is above the

powers of nature and not subject to its rhythm. That's why all
the other Gods have goddesses at their sides—an indication
that they too are involved in the creative process.

Next he is called *the living* God because his particular characteristic is to give life, that is, he has the ability and desire
to transfer man from death to life. Israel came to know its
God, Yahweh, in the deliverance from Egypt at the time of
the exodus. They came to know him as a savior, a redeemer.
He transfers people from prison to freedom, from oppression
to happiness, and that is, after all, from death to life. This is
his very own essence. Little by little we shall see this more
clearly, and I hope to be able to repeat much more illustra-
tively at the end of our meetings what I am now telling you.
What we said the last time about Samson was actually an illustration of this. In the great crisis of the seventh century
B.C. when the northern kingdom, Israel, was destroyed, the
people of little Juda reflected on God's nature and reminded
each other of it: "He made himself known as our savior, saving us from the straits of Egypt and from other distress. We
now recall all kinds of figures in history to illustrate this. Samson too was a savior sent by God to liberate the people from
the occupation of the Philistines."

Objections to Samson?

*You call Samson a savior, but when you read the story you
find out what a louse he was. If the bible is supposed to be
for everyone, stories like this are bound to cause confusion.
To me, Samson is more like a criminal than a God-sent
person.*

Try to understand that those stories came into being in a
time when a people was fighting for its existence. They de-

lighted in tall tales in which deeds of tribesmen against the Philistines were exaggerated and were concentrated around one figure in order to boost the nation's morale. They could not use Christian norms that had yet to be established. Moreover, here especially, we should not be hypocritical. You can still remember from the war how American bombers flew over with all those trails behind them. They carried bombs for the Germans. Did we have any objections?

I thought it was wonderful that they came. We cheered! Yes, they were our saviors. But that was in time of war when much is allowed.

That's exactly what I mean! Try to understand those people in the bible. They went through times of war, and like us they were glad when they heard how the enemy was "clobbered."

Yes, but I think that the idea is that Samson was notoriously bad in his personal life . . .

Don't forget that the Samson whom we know came into being as a result of the imagination of the people. All those heroic deeds in which our Samson was so strong against the Philistines and which were related with so much fervor—all those heroic deeds made him in the end a very great personality. Because people recognized only Yahweh as the one behind all events, this great person, Samson, was regarded as being sent by God to save them.

But don't you think his death was suicide?

Maybe so, but they didn't clearly understand at that time that suicide is wrong. Nobody would be scandalized by the

story. Besides, in contrast to all the cruel things he did, several
redeeming qualities appeared. For example, there is the beautiful opening of the short prayer which Samson says before
he deals the Philistines the final blow which annihilated him
as well (see Jg. 16, 28). From this we can conclude something
which is typical of Israel's religious conviction: Yahweh is
close to everyone; he who calls on him will always be heard.
Our Christian prayer is also founded on this certainty.

*So we have to realize that our moral standards were not
then accepted and that they had a quite different idea of God.*

Moral standards were indeed different, but their standards
were high. What we can learn from those Israelites is the sense
of God being involved in everything. This was the reason I
suggested the story of David and Bathsheba for your reading
after you read the story of Samson.

But wasn't that mainly to compare the two kinds of stories?

Yes. I wanted to familiarize you with the great variety of
stories in the bible. There are numerous differences between
the two extremes: on the one hand we have descriptions
strongly influenced by imagination, and on the other we have
what I should like to call purely historical reports, relating
what somebody has actually seen and heard. The story of Samson comes close to the first kind. This story based on concrete
historical circumstances grew and was expanded in the imagination of the people. As an example of the other kind, we
mentioned the story of David, written by somebody who knew
him, or, at any rate, knew the circumstances at court and who
wrote about something that actually happened to this real-life
person. In this manner I hoped to give you an impression of
the riches the bible contains in its stories.

But in addition to this, I have another reason. I want you to have a closer look at the prophet Nathan, at the way he acts in the name of the Israelite God, as the keeper so to speak of "God's right" in Israel. The Israelites accepted the existence of their people in the following sense: Yahweh made himself known by saving a group of slaves from the destructive power of Eygpt. At the same time he claimed this group as his. They became his possession, his property, and they were completely subject to him. This "covenant" held a number of obligations for Israel. In the first place they were to recognize Yahweh alone as their lord and master and not look for salvation from any other power. At the same time and just as surely they were obliged to respect the rights of every other Israelite.

Why Exactly Ten Commandments?

Israel's obligations were established and formulated quite early in a direct manner easy to understand. One set of the obligations we know as the "Ten Commandments." Have you ever thought why exactly ten? Why not seven? So many things in the bible go in sevens. Or twelve? I've come up with an explanation that I want to put before you merely as a suggestion. The reason could be that every man has ten fingers. Moses, or whoever it may have been, put the fundamental laws for every Israelite together so that five could be counted on one hand and five on the other. It would take too long to analyze this extensively. Let me try to do it briefly.

The first five commandments talk about the absolute rights of God over men. Man may not honor any other gods. That means that he may not look for salvation from other powers, called "gods" in the ancient world.

Next, he may not produce any image of God. In those days they still thought the person to be somehow present in his image, as is still the case with many orientals. When I was staying in Jerusalem I once had a Dutch acquaintance visiting me. He liked to draw and paint. He wanted to draw a Bedouin, so I engaged one for him. But when the former understood what the proposition was, he didn't want any part of it. These people think the possessor of a portrait has the power to injure the subject by puncturing the picture with pins. For the picture *is* the man. In the same way the Jews felt that an image of God is almost like God himself. And precisely because Yahweh is "transcendent," which means higher than everything that one can think of or imagine, producing an image of him might create the impression that one can make use of him at will.

Further, Yahweh's name may not be used in vain. Those ancient people often used the name of their gods as a means of magic power. It was simply a matter of crying out his name a thousand times and he was bound to react. Yahweh, however, is perfectly free and independent of everything and everyone.

To keep the Sabbath deals with the fact that time belongs entirely to God. We donate one seventh of that time to him; one day a week, to indicate really that *all* time is his. This is somewhat like giving the first produce of the harvest to him to express the idea that in fact everything is his.

Finally, according to Israelite belief parents bear the same relationship to their children as God does to his people. God gave us our existence through them. Parents, then, are not ordinary people to their children. They are from a different order—from God's order which gives life. These five commandments enumerated on one hand describe the rights of God.

Now the other hand. From the beginning the commandment "Thou shalt not kill" was not referring to killing in time of war, nor to the killing after due process of law, but to independent, private, killing, or murder. Here the other

person's right to life is safeguarded. Then comes the law that
forbids stealing. Originally that probably meant the stealing
of a person, to enslave him, or to sell him as a slave. Here the
right to personal freedom is protected. Furthermore we have
the prohibition against divorce—and the positive right to be
married and have a family. There is also the prohibition
against bearing false witness, which preserves the right to a
good name. In the last commandment the human right to
property is secured. For in the early Israelite language the
word "covet" included the concept of actually taking something away.

So you see how these two series cover both the rights of God
and man and when the two hands are folded together, they
form a *unity*.

This is expressed magnificently in the story we recently
read. When David had Uriah killed in order to take his wife,
the prophet Nathan came and said, "You sinned against God!"
For he who abuses the rights of his neighbors, abuses God. The
covenant is broken. All sacrifices now are worthless.

In the first book of Kings you have a similar incident. In
chapter twenty (in some bibles 21) we read that Ahab, King
of Samaria, had a certain Naboth executed so that he might
add his vineyard to his own property. No sooner had he committed this crime than the prophet Elias came before him and
said, "Nothing doing!" God cannot permit that a member of
the group in which he is recognized as the Lord be deprived
of his rights.

But don't you think that in the Old Testament too much
stress is put on the stern God, rather than the loving God
as we would prefer to see him now?

No, absolutely not. One of my intentions and wishes is to
explain that this is the wrong picture. Yahweh was from the

beginning considered as the one who saves people from distress—he who saved the Israelites and made them his people.
As such he cannot bear that one Israelite should bring ill-for-
tune upon another member of the tribe. The wrong impression that many people have of God in the Old Testament originates from the fact that one often remembers only the bloody
stories, and then he thinks that Jesus is bringing something
quite new. These people think that the Old Testament must
be quite different than the New. But that isn't so. Jesus is one
in the line of Elias and of Nathan, the line which began with
Moses. What they had to do within that community—namely
to defend the rights of God and man against all passion and
selfishness—that very same thing Jesus had to accomplish for
all of mankind with full commitment of his own person, even
to supreme sacrifice.

Virtue Outside the Chosen People

The statement about the preparation for the appearance of
Christ brings something else to mind. When you read chapter
eleven of the second book of Samuel, it must have struck you
that Uriah in the course of this story is called the Hittite several times. Deliberate stress is put on the fact that he did not
belong to the chosen people. And thus we get a much greater
contrast. David, the greatest king of Israel, behaves far worse
than the other characters that appear. True, Bathsheba is vain
and unfaithful. But Uriah, the one who was not an Israelite,
displays a heart-warming fidelity and *integrity*.

Here we touch upon one of the reasons why the story of
David's crime was so powerfully described and never removed
by later generations that honored David so highly. Israel had
to hear over and over again that being chosen by Yahweh does
not give any guarantee; it does not make those people better

than others! You are chosen by the true God only to serve him and mankind.

You know that this was one of the favorite themes of Jesus' sermons. On the road to Jericho the chosen priest and Levite pass by the dying man, and the one who is charitable is not among the chosen ones, he is cursed—a Samaritan. In the Old Testament this theme occurs in the book of Jonah among others. I suggest this as our reading for the next time. Don't let the word "book" scare you. There are only four short chapters, a real "short story." The two versions of the Ten Commandments you can find in the twentieth chapter of Exodus and in the fifth chapter of Deuteronomy, after which you might read the first part of the nineteenth chapter of Leviticus.

THREE:
God Chooses Mankind

One doesn't particularly honor Christ by saying that Israel knew a cruel and stern God and that later Jesus came to bring something absolutely new, namely a God of love, the Father of all mankind. This isn't true. From the very beginning Israel knew God as its savior from distress and death. It also knew that to injure one's fellow man was a sin against God. But soon a new understanding developed with this evergrowing knowledge: Israel had been "chosen" by God for the purpose of revealing his love of mankind. For those Jews who could not accept that serving role, the "short story" of Jonah was written.

So we see that the Gospel was already in preparation before Christ. That is why Christians can feel akin to the people speaking in the Old Testament.

I've noticed that several people in our group still don't see what all of this has to do with their daily lives. We want to read the bible in order to become better Christians. It's still not clear how we're supposed to accomplish that.

I hoped this might become easier to understand in the course of our conferences. However, let me now try to answer this fundamental question.

We start with the knowledge that the bible was brought forth in history. The book contains a great many witnesses to a certain way of life that developed in human history—namely the experience of reality as it was found among the Israelites, and later within the Christian Church. And because we as the faithful also accept and live in accordance with this reality, just as the people in the bible did, there is a connection between us and the bible. That is why the bible can "mean" something to us.

The reason why the Israelites stood out among the other peoples of their era may be summarized in three points.

God, the Covenant and Mankind

Point one: The Israelites set one power—one God—above everything. During the earliest times of the ancient world man considered the powers of nature to be divine. The sun was a god, the moon, the wind, and the water were gods. So for those people who lived in close contact with nature there was a vast number of gods. I remember a book which listed 3300 Babylonian gods. We also know of a Pharaoh who every year threw a letter into the Nile with the request to the Nile god to flood the Nile in the next year; otherwise the land would dry up. Every man knew that he was involved in that world of divine powers, all of whom had conflicts of their own. Man knew he was the toy in those conflicts. The people of Israel confess there is one God, one person rising above all powers of nature. This nation confesses: "We know that the divine power is one and personal because it has entered into a relationship with us, that relationship has become personal *for us*." With this declaration Israel takes a unique position in the ancient world. Point one gives us a striking comparison between the Babylonian story of the flood and the story found in the bible. We shall save this till later.

Now, point two: Israel did borrow something from the world around her, the notion of "covenant." By this the Israel-ites could describe the unique relationship to God which they enjoyed. In the years between 2000 and 1000 B.C. the Assyri-ans, Hittites, and Egyptians were large and powerful nations. When the ruler or feudal lord of such a nation had done some-thing for a smaller state, a vassal, then a "covenant" was made between him and the vassal according to a definite de-sign and specified rules. In such a covenant, which was always written, the feudal lord began by introducing himself, "I am so-and-so." Then he mentioned what he had done for the vas-sal, "I granted you such-and-such a favor!" Then came the basic demand, "You must therefore be loyal to me." After that a number of concrete terms of the covenant followed: release of prisoners, no covenants with others, military assistance, and so on. Finally came the supplication to the gods and formulas of blessing and cursing, "You will be blessed if you keep the covenant and cursed when you break it." Copies of covenants were put into the temple of both the feudal lord and the vas-sal.

So then, Israel applied this notion of covenant taken from political life to her relationship with God: Yahweh made such a covenant with us. He offered it to us because of a great fa-vor, his rescuing us from Egypt. That is his great boon. That is also the way he introduces himself, *"I am Yahweh, your Lord; I brought you out of the land of Egypt."* Then the basic demand in the Ten Commandments, "You shall have no other gods before me," followed by other demands, each carrying its own blessing or curse. This then is point two: Israel lives with God in a covenant relationship.

Point three I will treat very briefly. During the time of the kings when there were two states, Israel and Judah, a number of things happened, two of which I will mention. First of all, the people began to realize that the covenant was only a starting point. Yahweh's great purpose is to draw all nations together under the covenant. When all people follow the example which the Israelites were to give in recognizing Yahweh, thus respecting each other without killings and robbings, then world peace would come into being. Yahweh started with this small nation so that he might bring to pass within it what he wants to accomplish with all mankind. So the purpose of the covenant is to begin a procedure, to set a plan in motion so that all mankind eventually will grow into one happy community living in peace with one another. This is *one* way in which the faith of Israel was developing under the kings.

Second, the Jews continued to exist in spite of periods of unfaithfulness. Largescale national catastrophies occurred. Then the prophets said, "These disasters occur because you have broken the covenant, and so the curse has come upon you. Our benefactor demanded fidelity, and you did not fulfill that demand." Their unfaithfulness brought about the annihilation of the northern state, the deportation of Judah, and the exile in Babylon. Then it seemed as if the covenant was broken indeed, as if Yahweh had annulled it. But new prophets arose who said, "Yahweh has been our savior and benefactor since the days in Egypt, destruction cannot be his last word. His fidelity is stronger than your infidelity." Because of this belief, the people continued to exist after the exile as a community of Jews with Jerusalem as their center.

Christ the Apogee

These were a few main points of the age-old Israelite faith. About the year 28 of our calendar, Jesus of Nazareth entered

this picture. Just like the prophets and teachers of old, he made
known the demands and promises of God. But he did it in a
more radical manner. To recognize God as lord and master
of your life and be sensitive to the needs of your fellow men,
you must "lose your own self." Only by doing this do we give
God due honor. This manner of preaching was bound to clash
with the way the Pharisees practiced their faith. Their piety was
utterly selfish and as much an assault on God's majesty as an
insult to their fellow men. In line with what happened to earlier prophets who clearly proclaimed God's demands, Jesus
was eliminated. But then he could fully reveal the real nature
of the God of Israel. After his resurrection he joined his disciples and made it very clear that God is the real savior, and
that death cannot be the last word. Thus we see his disciples,
with the Christian people gathered around them as the
Church, living in dedication to the same God, knowing that
no distress can last forever. We as Christians are involved in
this process, this plan of salvation which began to be revealed
in ancient Israel as being directed toward all mankind.

*Well, that's quite a mouthful! Do you mean you can illus-
trate your third point by the book of Jonah? Was it written
during the time of the kings?*

No, it was written after the exile, probably sometime in the
fourth century or thereabout when Nineveh had already become a legendary city. You noticed perhaps that I called the
people "Israelites" during the early centuries, and "Jews" only
after the exile. The "remnant" of the tribe of Judah that returned from Babylon formed a province in and around Jerusalem. This province was called "Jehud" by the Persian conquerors, and later "Judea" by the Greeks and Romans. This
Jewish community had to try to hold its own against the influences of foreign conquerors. Many of them were inclined

to see their own group as the ultimate as far as God's interest in the world was concerned. They expected and prayed fervently that God might destroy all other nations—and some texts of the prophets seemed indeed to announce just that.

Israel a "Beachhead"

This selfish narrow-mindedness, so completely against the spirit of Yahweh, was counteracted by the Jew who wrote the short story of Jonah. He followed the tradition of the prophets who saw only a beginning in God's covenant with Israel. From this nation a blessing was to go forth to all other nations. I sometimes compare it in my lectures with a beachhead —although it may sound a little militaristic. When the Allies prepared to invade Germany they arrived at the Rhine with all the force they could muster, establishing a beachhead there. Next they gained some territory inside Germany itself, and from there they set out to conquer the rest. God began like this with Israel; "With this I shall start and from here I shall conquer all of mankind." Now when God conquers it means that he has the well-being of men at heart. So Israel was only the beginning. Jesus of Nazareth completely fulfilled this task of Israel in himself.

In the New Testament then, are you saying that we should recognize the whole Old Testament?

The New Testament consists really of witnesses of the first generation of Christians. The people who were living when Jesus lived wrote down their recollections which we call the New Testament. But never forget that when Jesus himself spoke about the bible, he meant our Old Testament. When the apostles in their letters mentioned the bible they also meant the Old Testament. The New Testament did not appear in book form until the second century after Christ. The first Christians, then, read only the Old Testament—entirely in terms of their own experience.

So we should really read the Old Testament with the New in mind?

Yes, but it is not so much a question of having *the book,* which we call the New Testament, in mind. Rather, we should approach the Old Testament in our New Testament *faith.* What we are doing here is merely talking about the bible. But, how best to express this . . . ? Let me give an example. A television announcer reads all sorts of news with a sober face —that's as it should be. One day with an indifferent expression on his face, he reads that somewhere a bomber has taken off to drop an atom bomb on New York in ten minutes. Everyone in New York who hears it exclaims, "Oh, that's me! That announcement is meant for me!" Similarly, we can read the bible soberly, like an old history book, uninvolved; *it does not concern me.* But *the* occasion at which you should read the bible is when God speaks the clearest to you and when you are taken into the same covenant. That is at holy Mass, when we gather on Sundays for the eucharistic feast. We are in the same situation as were the first Christians. Jesus comes with his message from God as a savior and benefactor, but also with his demand to give ourselves and to love our neighbors, everybody, even our enemies. Then we also hear the joyous tiding that God shall prove to be stronger than all misery. And with that knowledge we once again begin a new week. With this message we can again face our troubles. This shows that not everybody needs to read the bible at home. The place where the bible should be read as it was intended—as an address or a message—is at the eucharistic feast where we come to hear the voice of God, and to become involved in it, to say "Amen" to it!

Then it's not so terribly important whether you can place all of it historically or not?

No, that's not terribly important. However, as we said in the beginning: It is good to know what the writer of a certain piece meant and *where* he belonged in the long and varied history of a people's way of life . . .

The Story of Jonah

Take the case of Jonah. The author of this book lived among Jews who expected the imminent downfall of the other nations. They didn't understand that even the most radical threats of the prophets against the nations had risen from the concern of a God who was ready to forgive and to let them begin over again at the first sign of repentance. Moreover, they had forgotten that they themselves had remained deaf again and again to their prophets who were trying to bring them to conversion. The author of this story pictures their attitude in the person of Jonah. All the other people in the story are agreeable and friendly: the pagan sailors, the king and the inhabitants of Nineveh which was the capital of Assyria, the arch enemy of Israel. Jonah, the Jew, alone is despicable. He withdraws from the service to the heathen for which God has chosen him—read: "God has chosen Israel." Then God mobilizes nature in the form of a storm and a huge fish which do obey him, to place Jonah where God wants him. And when the inhabitants, upon the first warning of Jonah, do what the Jews in all those centuries of preaching by the prophets never managed to do, Jonah becomes angry. When they are converted and do penance in sackcloth and ashes and when as a result God saves the city, Jonah cries, *"Wouldn't you know it! You are merciful. Phooey! It doesn't matter now if I die!"* And God appears to be merciful toward this miserable small human being and points with mild irony to his love for all people, even for their cattle.

We see that a good insight into the situation of the author can greatly clarify the purpose and details of his stories. We also see the connection with the New Testament better. Jesus had to fight against the same jealous narrow-mindedness, and he too tried to expose this attitude in striking stories. Think of the workers in the vineyard. "Are you angry because I do good?" It wasn't coincidental that Jesus liked to quote from the story of Jonah so often. Really quite a bit of what we think of as belonging to the gospels was already present in the Old Testament.

Law and Love

Does this hold true for the Ten Commandments also? Are they still to be adhered to, even though Christ has come?

Yes, the message of the Gospel has been forecast in that life under the covenant which the Ten Commandments expressed. Unfortunately translations of the commandments often sound indirect. Here we meet a peculiarity of old Israel. In the texts of the oriental treaties which we discussed, the king is always the only one who acts. Behind him, hardly visible, is the shapeless mass of his people. In the covenant between God and Israel each member of the nation is personally addressed in the singular, "I am the Lord, your God, . . . *You* shall not kill, *you* shall not covet . . ." So in Israel a start was made with—I almost hesitate to say it—a democracy; however, this word has been abused. At any rate, its people were seen and accepted as a society of independent and responsible individuals with the king being bound by the law as much as the man in the street. We saw this in the case of David.

You may say "democracy," but when the announcement of the commandments was made it was accompanied by thunder and lightning. That is not very democratic.

That's exactly why the word isn't right. "Theocracy" would be better. This means that all authority rests in God. Such was the case in Israel, and therefore all Israelites were to have equal rights. In the sight of God no human being is more or less than the other. The Israelites were to show this by a perfect brotherhood among themselves—and the Ten Commandments were the means to bring them to this goal.

We shall see how Christ lived all of this much more radically. More than anyone before him, was he taken up with God's majesty. Therefore he understood better what people like the author of Jonah felt, that before God all people are equal, Jew and Gentile alike. Thus Jesus broke through the barrier of Israel and made the Ten Commandments universal.

Better still, he rendered them superfluous. Jesus demanded total surrender to God whereby man puts himself in God's hands, "losing himself," as we indicated awhile back. He who accomplishes this has no need to murder, to steal from or to slander another person in order to uphold himself and satisfy his desires. That is exactly what he has been freed from— himself and his desires. In obeying Christ we have become free to answer his call coming to us from our needy brothers. This explains Paul's cherished remark that the Ten Commandments and any other laws do not apply if a person really lives in the love of God.

But with this we have become involved in the New Testament, and I want to discuss the Old Testament a little longer. We'll understand the actions of Jesus better if we first learn something about the prophets who preceded him. I suggest that you examine chapters five and six of the book Isaiah.

FOUR:
God's Wrath and Mercy

Last time we mentioned in passing the Babylonian flood story. We shall now compare it with the biblical version of the same story. Then we shall take up the main topic, the fifth and sixth chapters of Isaiah with a sketch of the historical background of the pronouncements gathered together in there. The greatest power in the world of that time, Assyria, threatened small Judah with its enormous and swift armies. But the prophet's faith made him understand that it was really Yahweh who sent them. He, the God living on small Zion, was *the* king who holds the destiny of the world in his hand. He used the Assyrian armies to chastise his people. He expected brotherly love among the people representing him on earth, but the only things he found were injustice and crime. His deep disappointment was expressed by the prophet's threatening cries, "Woe to you. . . ." In associating with this people as "the Holy One of Israel," the divine majesty appears to be capable of great concern for the people, capable of expecting results, being disillusioned.

How Israel Pictured the Flood

In our last session we spoke about Israel's conception of God as a unique phenomenon in the ancient world. The Israelites saw everything they derived from that world with the eyes of faith. This becomes obvious in the biblical version of a story that circulated in Mesopotamia, long before Israel existed, about a flood from which one man and his family were saved. This flood story in Mesopotamia was taken into a larger unit, the so-called "Gilgamesh epic," one of the most beautiful literary accomplishments of mankind.

In the ancient world there was no strict separation between the divine and the human. As king of the city of Uruk, the hero of the story—Gilgamesh—was not an ordinary human being. He was two-thirds divine and one-third human in nature. He, with his friend Enkidu, met with all sorts of adventures. When Enkidu died, Gilgamesh became concerned and troubled with the prospect of the fact that he also must die. He set out to look for immortality and came upon a man called Utnapishtim, which means "He-found-life." He was privileged to live forever and he showed Gilgamesh a means to receive life without end. He told him of an herb growing deep down in the water which if eaten would confer immortality. Gilgamesh dived for the herb, found it and took it to his town Uruk. He wanted to let all the people in his town eat the herb, called, "As-an-old-man-you-shall-become-young-again." On the long journey home he stopped to bathe in a cool pond beside the path and what happened? A snake appeared and ate the herb, thereupon becoming young and shedding its old skin. Gilgamesh had to accept the fact that he would remain mortal.

Utnapishtim, or "He-found-life," had previously told Gilgamesh how he himself had received this privilege. He said that he was the hero of the flood and related the story, which I will only summarize here:

In the course of a noisy meeting the gods decide to flood the entire world. One of the gods, named Ea, wants to reveal this to a human. He doesn't speak directly to Utnapishtim, but whispers through the wall of a thatched hut in which the latter is sleeping the words: "Build an ark." This the man does; and all of the descriptions of the boat duplicate those in the bible story: measurements, tar, and so on. Then comes the downpour and the waters begin to rise. All the gods become panicky. I quote the text: "They searched for shelter in heaven above; like dogs they crouched against the wall." The earth stays covered with water for seven days and then the ark hits a mountain. Utnapishtim lets a pigeon fly out, but it returns; then a swallow, and it returns. But the raven does not come back. Then he offers a sacrifice. (Realize now that the sacrifices offered by mankind provided the food for the gods.) The story continues: "The gods smelled the sweet odor and swarmed like flies around the person offering the sacrifice."

Is there any connection between the bible story and Gilgamesh?

Yes, but the story from the epic is much older. It was such a beautiful story that when it reached Israel the people wanted to tell it there too, but they could not accept it with such a beginning and end! For once you believe in only one power which guides everything, a power which is just and noble, it becomes necessary to alter the story. A catastrophe in nature can only be caused by the one God. Man cannot help but see it as a punishment. If such a calamity strikes all of humanity, then you must first relate how all people must have been sinful. The only reason a person is saved from such a punishment must be that he is just and that he *"found favor in the eyes of the Lord."* (Gen. 6, 8).

Is it possible that these two versions are separate accounts of the same historical event?

I don't think so. Mesopotamia was time and again afflicted by sudden and destructive floods. The survivors must have been surprised everytime they survived. When a grandfather would say, "This is nothing compared to the flood that I witnessed in my youth; it really covered the entire world," a little boy would ask, "But Grandpa, what about you?" Upon which grandfather would tell of the warning from the gods and how he then built the ark . . . Perhaps it's too simple to put like this. Maybe I do this in opposition to those people who want to discover traces of "the" bible flood in excavations, and to those who write third-rate books which keep on grinding out the idea that the bible flood actually happened. Those who cling to the idea of one flood as proof that the bible stories do so in spite of the fact that scientists are convinced that the sand layers which were found have nothing to do with flooding but are the result of sand drifts.

But haven't there been expeditions fully equipped to find the ark of Noah?

That is done by people with a fantastic imagination, or by fakes. Don't ever contribute money to such experiments. These people don't take the biblical authors as they should. The authors were trying to give an expressive illustration of their belief in God who punishes evil and who gives grace to whomever he chooses.

Is this then the real meaning of the story?

One can hardly speak about *the* meaning of a story, certainly not if it is a biblical story, as if such a story could have only one meaning. If you want to proclaim a certain thesis, you explain its terminology, and then everybody knows exactly what is meant. However it's different with a story. That's why a philosopher, when he touches upon the innermost realities, leaves his theories behind and tries his luck with a story. A story can be charged with all kinds of symbols. It furnishes a better picture of a given reality with all its varying aspects than concepts and definitions do.

The story of the flood served several different purposes in Israel. First, it was good listening material because it was so dramatic and impressive. Next, it gave insight into the world-embracing power of Yahweh. Furthermore, during the first period of written literature, after David, it was put into a larger context—what we might call the earliest version of Genesis. An author wanted to show how evil and sin spread. First, he described the sin of Adam and Eve. Immediately after came the story of Cain and Abel, for, the author reasoned, if you no longer recognize God as your Lord and you want to be your own master, the first thing you are going to do is kill your brother. The murdering continues and Lamech avenges himself seventy-seven times. Adding a fragment of an old myth, he tells that the sons of God keep company with the daughters of men. This is summit of evil, and the flood follows . . . But I stepped over into Genesis, and we intended to talk about the book Isaiah, didn't we?

Isaiah and World Politics

I think you have read chapters five and six of Isaiah. I should like to suggest a division into four parts.

The fifth chapter, verses one to seven: The song of the vineyard. You must have been impressed by this profound piece of poetry. It ends in God's reproach to his people. "I expected fruits (justice and charity), and I did not receive any such fruits."

Chapter five, verses eight to twenty-five: These verses are a series of "woes": *Woe to those who join house to house;* they are the big property owners. *Woe to those . . . who acquit the guilty for a bribe. Woe to those who mock God,* and so on. There are a few *"therefores"* among them: therefore God shall punish his people . . .

Chapter five, verses twenty-six to thirty: This is the impressive description of an enormous charging army. We see it storming ahead, but we are not told whose army it is.

Chapter six: This is the vision of the prophet who sees God as "the" king and who gets his assignment from him.

To understand these passages fully we must look at their historical background, keeping in mind the geographical aspects. The history of Israel and the development of its faith were determined by the geographical position of Palestine. What happened in that narrow corridor between the impassable desert and the Mediterranean Sea was always dependent upon the whims of the powers at both ends of the corridor—Egypt in the south and Mesopotamia or Syria in the north. David was able to build a great kingdom partly because at that time (around 1000 B.C.) there were no important powers either in Egypt or in the land between the Euphrates and Tigris rivers. That's why David could subdue the surrounding peoples and countries: Ammon, Moab, Edom, the Philistines and, northward, Damascus, Hamath, and so on. After Solomon's death this empire broke up again into its many parts—among which were Israel and Judah.

In the ninth century the power of Assyria was developing in Mesopotamia, with world hegemony as its goal. The campaigns westward to the Mediterranean coast became more and more frequent. Of great importance was the year 745 B.C. when Tiglatpileser III mounted the throne of Assyria and introduced a new strategy. Instead of taxing the conquered people he deported their leading class to the far ends of his world territories in order to destroy their national existence. Don't forget that in that world this meant also that the national god was defeated and deposed. The most that any conquered people could expect was that the statue of their chief deity might arrive as a trophy in some Assyrian temple, and thus it would be clear that the god Assur had proved to be the stronger one.

Who Dominates the Course of History?

Because of the new Assyrian policy, a problem arose for the two little kingdoms, Israel and Judah: "Who will prove to be the stronger, god Assur or God Yahweh?" If you realize that the calling of Isaiah occurred in 740 B.C., when the news of this new policy was beginning to reach the two small countries, when it was becoming clear that the very existence of the people and of Yahweh was at stake, then you may understand the full impact of that tremendous vision: the true ruler of the world is Yahweh, the God of small Zion. This is the historical significance of the vision of Yahweh as *the* king.

The prophet asserts that Israel's God is guiding world history for the benefit of his people. This is an almost foolish statement of faith. It is as if someone in Albania should arise to make this statement, *"The whole Soviet Union really exists to serve us; everything they do centers around us Albanians."* In the same manner Isaiah says that the Assyrians, the enormous armies that storm ahead, are called upon by Yahweh to punish his people. This you see in verse twenty-six of chapter five: *"He will whistle for [a nation] from the ends of the earth."* In other words, he directs this enormous Assyrian power in order to chastise his people.

Because the vineyard did not bring forth good fruit?

Yes, exactly. Israel did not remain true to its vocation. This is illustrated in the song of the vineyard. God is being compared to a farmer who takes care of his crop and who expects a good harvest. And what does he receive? A crop failure. And in verse seven this is expressed very forcefully. The Hebrew here is almost impossible to translate with its play on words, but everybody tries to do it. It reads: "God expected *mishpat,* which means justice, loyalty, honesty in courts. And what does he receive? *mishpakh,* some sort of injustice and violence accompanied by bloodshed. He also expected *sedaqa,* which is loyalty among the people. What is the result? *Seäqà* which is the clamor of the unjustly oppressed.

In my translation it says: "He expected good government, but look, it was a reign of terror! Law-abiding people, but look, they abused the law."

This is a good way of saying it. Only the last Hebrew word does not show in the translation. For what God hears is the screaming for help from the people who are unjustly oppressed. I myself tried to translate it: *"Justice he expected to keep but look, the oppressed weep."* Retaining the rhyme, the meaning of *seäqà* stands out a little bit more, and the connection with "woes" is preserved. It had been common knowledge since ancient times that Yahweh did not want one man to oppress the other. It was the very *seäqà,* the clamoring of Israel, which made him act so violently against Egypt (see Exod. 3, 7-9). Here the prophet really speaks from within the structure of the covenant.

Had northern Israel already been destroyed when he spoke those words?

That happened in 721, or during the ministry of Isaiah. This must have been from 740 to 700 B.C. Note, however, that such a book attributed to a prophet consists of all sorts of unconnected statements remembered and gathered by his pupils after his death. Some of those we can place in order somewhere in those forty years, others we cannot. Later we shall see the same thing happen with the gospels.

At the end of chapter six we read that "a holy seed remains as its root." So was some part of Israel saved?

Yes, some part of the northern kingdom, Israel, remained after 721. This became the starting point of the later-occurring Samaritans. But that is a story in itself. In any case, about one-tenth of the people of God was left in 721, namely the country of Judah. Later they were decimated also, so that only a small number was left. But God never destroys, as you ought to know from our last discussion, precisely because he is more faithful than his unfaithful people. His last word is never a word of destruction; in the end he always brings salvation.

Was it not precisely to show his greatness that a small part remained, because he does go on with the small remnant that was left? Or do I express myself the right way?

No, you phrased it correctly. You touch here upon something mysterious, but I prefer to come back to this later. In any case, what you see happening here will later culminate in Christ. For the moment remember from chapters five and six of Isaiah the two things that go together. First, God is so great and so tremendously majestic that you must die if you see him only for a fraction of a second. At the same time, the divine majestic being can be disappointed in his expectations. This high and overpowering majesty had hoped that Israel would represent him in this world through justice and love, and he was disappointed in that hope. These two ideas you must remember, and also this point: the faith of the prophet, which really is our faith too, is that the divine majesty takes an interest in those with whom he has a covenant. He does hear me when I call on him. This I know for certain, and this I believe, and so do you.

Once I stayed at the home of someone who didn't share our faith. He was extremely hospitable and a very fine man. One day he told his wife, "This Luke will of course want to say his prayers before meals; that is customary in his circles." When we talked about this the next day he said, "I cannot understand how you dare to bother the Supreme Being with the fact of eating a sandwich." I'll never forget that. For exactly with that statement he characterized our faith: God is interested in everything concerning the person with whom he has a personal relationship. Jesus exaggerates to make the point: "God, your heavenly father, is interested even in the number of hairs on our heads . . ."

Our faith was once beautifully expressed by Toon Hermans, a famous Dutch comedian and performer. At the end of a Christmas show he said, "You know, people, on Monday you get up and you say, 'Darn it!' But you know what you should do? You should say, 'Thank you very much!'" This is the attitude of a man who has faith, who considers everything that happens to him as a personal gesture, a gift. And so you are grateful for the sandwich you are about to eat. You don't have to say grace at every meal. Don't unduly try to prove that you are a Catholic by praying at every meal. However, it is very true that saying grace before meals has a very deep meaning associated with our existence as believers.

After Isaiah I should like to discuss how Jesus acted as a prophet. Therefore, I suggest the reading of the Gospel of Luke, chapter thirteen.

FIVE:
The Problem of Evil

Chapter thirteen of Luke's Gospel begins with a conversation between Jesus and the people about the guilt of some Galileans who had recently been killed and whose blood Pilate had mixed with their sacrifices. Jesus asked whether those people, as well as the eighteen persons who had lost their lives in Jerusalem when a tower caved in, were more guilty than those who were spared. This question gives us reason to stay with the Old Testament a bit longer. The discussion of a problem which kept so many Jews wondering can bring many texts closer to us, especially in the book of Job. Moreover it can give us some idea of the manner in which revelation took place.

No Reckoning after This Life

The problem of guilt and punishment had particular pertinence in the case of the Galileans since it brought up the matter of God's justice in allowing death to befall his people when they were on their way to the temple, or perhaps even at the moment they were honoring him in the temple by sacrificing the best of their possessions.

Before the coming of Christ, questions like these worried many people. They were especially disturbing because those who spoke in the Old Testament (except in the very last works) did not yet know about the just reward or punishment of human deeds in the hereafter. They did not see the horizon of human life extending beyond this earthly existence. They didn't know of any reckoning after death.

But I wonder, if they didn't know of a life hereafter, why didn't they live more recklessly without reservations?

You imply that the good or bad way of living depends on whether or not a person believes in life after death. I think the Israelites and Jews saw it in a different way. They believed that God is the master of this life *now at this moment,* and that serving God means obeying him in this life. It means living in communion with him, as servants live in obedience to their lord. Whether there is a life hereafter is not very important, but to serve God *now* is important. God wants everybody to respect the right of his fellow men—according to the last five of the Ten Commandments. This means, as we have seen, that he alone be recognized as lord and master. (Think of the first five of the Ten Commandments.) Everything in life centers around this. All of existence is included in this.

I think that's great. However, we always tend to think a little about life hereafter in trying to live well.

And for a good reason! Yet it is good for us to mingle with those people of the Old Testament. They serve as a warning against seeing religion merely as a means for future reward.

The Israelites that lived during the era of David and the kings that succeeded him saw the life of an individual limited to earthly existence. There was believed to be some form of continuance of existence, but it did not deserve the name "life." After death man arrived in the underworld, and then existed only as a shade, or as literally translated: a "weakling." Man thought of the underworld as a space without light or joy or happiness where God could not be praised. There was no longer any distinction between people; king and slave, the good man and the bad one—all ended up there. So after this life there was really nothing which could be called life, for life meant to the Israelites all these things together: happiness, health, a certain amount of wealth, a large family, a good name, and so on. If anything of that entity was taken away, men prayed that God might give back life, life in its fullness. However, this life was limited by time. At a certain moment it was finished, and then man landed in the underworld as a shade. *Sheol,* as this world was called, was seen as some sort of an immense grave, of which the individual tomb was the vestibule. Yet at the same time the believing Israelite saw all of reality, and thus also everything pertaining to human life, as being under the dominion of Yahweh, the one, just and merciful God. If someone sinned, it was believed, then God must punish him for it during his lifetime. If someone was good and pious, then his reward from God could only come in this life, in the form of prosperity, a good name, and so on. When a person had lived a full life,—when he had reached 80 or 90 years of age—then he was said to enjoy "the fullness of years." He had received his share in that wonderful relationship of God with Israel and then went contented to the underworld. There *was* no other way.

Facts Contradict Dogma

Apparently the Israelites accepted this concept for many long centuries. But sometime in the seventh century B.C., near the decline of the kingdom of Judah, we notice in the biblical texts that people did not so readily believe in this concept of life any longer. They began to see that the facts did not always tally with their notions. We come, for example, across the famous King Josiah who reigned from about 640 B.C. and who did a great deal for the people of God by his religious reforms. He also improved the general welfare of the people, the economy and the army. In 609, Josiah engaged in a battle against the Egyptians and was killed in action, long before he reached *the fullness of years*. If untimely death was supposed to be punishment, what sin had this outstanding man then committed?

At this time the prophet Jeremiah was also on the scene. All his life this man fulfilled his difficult duty to speak the word of God to the people. He experienced a tremendous amount of resistance. People from his own village wanted to murder him. The king, the authorities, the people—everybody was against him. He truly had a very hard life. But he deserved to be treated differently. Hence his bold question: *"Righteous are thou, O Lord, when I complain to thee: yet I would plead my case before thee. Why does the way of the wicked prosper?"* (Jer. 12, 1-2)

The problem became more explosive during and after the exile. After the downfall of the people and of their holy city, the Judeans were captive in distant Babylonia as "displaced persons." Under such circumstances people begin to think about their lot in life. Even the children that were born there said later to their parents, "Because you sinned in the past we are here. How can that be just?"

In the following centuries the Jewish community was constantly subject to foreign powers: first the Persians, later the Greeks. It was occupied territory like many European countries during World War II. What happens in such a situation? If you collaborate with the oppressor you are treated well;

you get good jobs and all sorts of opportunities to increase your wealth. But if you are true patriots, then you always get the worst end of the deal. The same things happened at that time. The Jews who cooperated with the Persians and later with the Greek conquerors were doing fine in business and were favored before the courts. But the patriots, the Jews who courageously stuck to their traditions and laws and who avoided contacts with the foreigners, had it rough. And so the problem of a just reckoning became more difficult.

There were Jews who said, "The dogma is clear and it remains clear. If misfortune comes, it must be a punishment for sins committed. For God is unfailingly just. He rewards the good and punishes the bad, and that must take place during one's lifetime. If a person is doing well and continues to do well, then he has proved himself to be a good man."

The Book of Job

To contradict this simplified opinion about the human lot somebody went into action and wrote the Book of Job. The author describes his main character, Job, in the most beautiful terms that Hebrews could use to describe a human being: *"He was blameless and upright, one who feared God and turned away from evil"* (Job. 1, 1). Consequently he was a man of great wealth. He is pictured as a biblical patriarch with large herds of animals. He possessed seven thousand sheep, five hundred she-asses and a great number of camels. He also had seven sons and three daughters who lived rather merrily. Every brother regularly invited all of his brothers and sisters for a celebration. At the end of such a feast, Job called them together and offered a sacrifice for possible sins that they might have committed during the feast—so perfectly pious and correct was Job.

The author was living at a time when men began to surmise that the evil in the world might perhaps be caused by a supernatural force whom they named Satan; of course they placed him under God in rank. After the author gives a view of Job and his way of life, he pictures a scene on an elevated stage, where Satan appears in the council chamber of God. Satan gets permission to try Job's attitude and faithfulness toward God.

When Job is tried to the utmost, three friends come to sit with him for seven days, unable to utter even one word. Then Job bursts out in a plaintive cry, and he curses the day that he was born. The conversations with his friends follow (chapters 4-27). Neither Job nor they are aware that Satan has been injected into the scene. The friends think that Job must have brought his misfortune upon himself. Why then doesn't he confess his sins and contritely turn back to God? Then God will bless him again. Job passionately protests and in his answers to his friends he often turns to God directly. This dialogue is a tremendous piece of literature. But it is biblical poetry, which means that it has many repetitions and that it centers about the same themes; so for us people in a western civilization it is rather difficult to read. At first, one should read only a few small fragments. After an entirely detached song of praise about God's wisdom (chapter 28), there follow three chapters in which Job speaks about his former life. Chapter thirty-one reveals explicitly the very high morals of the Jewish society. After the "dare" with which this chapter ends, one can best skip the later added meditations of Elihu and look at the grand answer of God (beginning with chapter 38). One can see that the author treated the problem in a true biblical manner, not by reasoning but by illustration with a specific central figure, a concrete person. We have no idea what circles of readers the book reached. At any rate many Jews kept on struggling with the still-open questions. It was not long before Christ that we find the first indications that the Jews were beginning to believe in some sort of a retribution after death—a resurrection.

Retribution Comes in Sight

We can only guess how this broadening of insight came about. The process was long and intricate; we do not have enough factual material to be able to describe it. All kinds of experiences and motives played a part in it. Especially influential were the experiences which truly pious people had in their communication with God through prayer. Some of the Psalms are proof of this. There were also some very concrete facts which made it impossible to retain the old dogma. One of the most important among these facts was the struggle of the Maccabees. During their battles, for the sake of both Israel and God, many young men were killed. Their untimely death could hardly be seen as a punishment. On the contrary, if ever anyone should be part of the final revelation of God's glory, of the Kingdom of God, then it should be those young men who sacrificed their lives for this cause.

During that time, about the year 165 before Christ, the Book of Daniel was written; here the belief in a future resurrection is mentioned for the first time (12, 2).

But I remember some texts of the Psalms in which hope for an eternal life is expressed. Weren't those written much earlier?

Yes, that's true, but the Psalms originate in various periods, between the tenth and the fourth centuries before Christ. That's why different stages of the described development of viewpoints are represented in them. In Psalm 36 (37) for example, which is a kind of educational poem, the author explicitly states the old opinion that the sinner undoubtedly will be punished during his lifetime and that the just man will receive his reward. He says approximately: "Young people, you see that the sinner is doing well, but believe me—I am a man with experience!—his luck will not last. One of these days he will come to his downfall, rest assured. And the just man seems to be doing badly now, but if he keeps faith in Yahweh he will have a long and happy life." In other Psalms people speak with a conviction acquired by prayer. This conviction became the essence of their lives. They are confident in their hopes that God will not allow death to end the intimate relationship between him and them. They seem to say: "Whatever happens, my death shall not be the end of my communication with God. That *cannot* be. He surely will know a way to save me from that dark and god-forsaken underworld so that I may be with him forever." This appears clearly expressed in Psalm 72 (73) and it is also vaguely indicated in other psalms, for example in 15 (16) and at the end of 16 (17).

Is it possible that the new viewpoint, in the time of the Maccabees, might have been influenced by contact with the Greeks?

There may have been some Greek influence, but this was not of a determining character. An Israelite and a Jew think of man as a whole. They had great difficulty imagining, as the Greek did, some kind of an independent soul which would be perfectly happy when finally freed from the chains of the body. A Jew could visualize man's happiness only on condition that man is a complete body and soul. Although there may certainly have been some Greek influence, it was more stimulating than determining.

*Was the belief in life hereafter, which developed so slowly,
influenced by the circumstances in which those good people
lived? They had to find a solution to the problem, so . . .*

That's undoubtedly correct. Only, those people didn't accept bare circumstances. They knew only God who governs
everything, who has everything in his hand. And if he is just
(and he is), then justice has to come to light sooner or later.
If it cannot be shown by material goods of this earthly life,
then justice will be done in another manner.

They were more altruistic?

Yes, in a way. They were especially concerned about God
and the revelation of his justice and mercy. They saw their
own lot connected with their mission of serving God. It's good
to remember, especially when you talk with your children,
that so many people were truly faithful, just and generous to
their fellow men without knowing there was a life hereafter.
For "to live well only because of a heavenly reward later on"
is very un-biblical and un-Christian.

In the history of Israel and Christ, everything centers
around the freeing of man from his egotism. By being open to
God and our neighbor we become happy. We may then speak
about a "reward" in the life hereafter (Christ himself does
this.), but it can hardly mean anything else than this: God
himself completes our redemption from the egotism which
prevented us from being completely happy here on earth.

In our day there is—and rightly so—a violent reaction
against that practice of our faith which stressed happiness
in the life hereafter so much that the very urgent problems of
this earth were neglected. Reactions always lead to onesided-
ness. And this is another reason why it is good to come in contact with biblical figures. They show us that God is our mas-

ter *now*. He comes now to us with his wishes, which he reveals not only in the scriptures and sermons but also through the situations in which we are living—our daily tasks, the needs of our fellow men, the necessity to help build a better world.

I suggest that you read some of the fragments from the book of Job in the light of what we have discussed.

> *Concerning Job, I really think God is having a strange conversation with Job, if I may describe it like that. I think God is using man to brag about him in front of Satan.*

Honestly, I never thought of that difficulty. It seems worthwhile to develop this a little further.

SIX:
Warnings and Threats

Satan is granted an audience at the heavenly court. God is clearly proud of the virtuous Job. Then Satan gets permission to try him. One of you found this shocking—God gambling with the happiness of a human being simply to be able to "brag" about him. We are going to study this difficulty in a wider context. The mystery we refer to by using the word "God," is infinitely high above us, and at the same time very close to us. The biblical stories and statements shed light on both "sides" of the mystery. Whoever sees God has to die—because God is so overpoweringly different from man. But at the same time God also walks in a garden, visits with Abraham, knows anger, joy and pity—is very close to man. He can make himself visible in our world only through people fully dedicated to him. Next we shall finally take up the study of Luke, chapter thirteen. There we shall discover something of Jesus' impassioned appeal to his people: his preaching was their very last chance.

God: Different, Yet Close to Man

You objected to the picture presented by the first chapters of Job. God seems to misuse the happiness of a human being for his own honor and glory. I would like to treat this, for it compels me to show in how many different ways the bible illustrates the mystery of God; this is important to everyone who reads it. I should like to give the answer in two parts. First there will be a general discussion, and then an examination of the statement as to whether or nor God can be pictured as "bragging" about a human being.

As for the first, we repeatedly saw how the Israelites were characterized by their extraordinary perception of the divine mystery. This perception has two opposing poles, two aspects that seem to exclude each other. Namely, God is infinitely far above man, inaccessible, inexpressible, totally different from man; at the same time he is extremely close, is actively present in everything, is involved in everything that happens in nature, in history, and in human life.

Even in the name with which they referred to God, the Israelites could hear these two aspects. In their alphabet, which contains only consonants, the name of God is spelled with the four letters Y H W H, which we pronounce "Yahweh."

Is that the same as Jehovah?

Yes, but that pronunciation isn't correct. The vowels that were inserted are wrong. This came about as follows. For several centuries before Christ, and even more so during his life, the Israelites had so much respect for the holy name that they avoided pronouncing it. In those times, as you may know, people always read aloud, never silently. When the Jews came to the four letters of the holy name, they pronounced the word "Adonai" which in Hebrew means "Lord." Some centuries after Christ the Jews added vowel-signs to the consonantal text of their Hebrew writings in order to safeguard their exact pronunciation. To the four consonants of the holy name, YHWH, they added the vowels of the word that should be read, Adonai. The first vowel of Adonai sounds like a mute *e,* the second like an *o,* the third like an *a*. Later Christians, unaware of the Jewish usage, naively combined those vowels with the consonants, and invented YeHoWaH. How the ancient Israelites vocalized the holy name is not entirely certain. Most scholars think that it was pronounced Yahweh.

In any case they heard in the name a form of the verb "to be," namely the third person singular of the present tense. The form "Yahweh" is just about equivalent to our "He is." First this indicated to them that God has no limits, no end, that he is infinite—boundless—he "is" without any qualification. To use the word "person" for example in reference to God, introduces a concept which is really too small, a limitation. Secondly the verb "to be" also had an active and dynamic character. "He is" meant also that he is everywhere and always present and actively involved.

Theology in the Form of a Story

Those two aspects or two opposite poles which the Israelites associated with the name Yahweh were also expressed in various statements and stories. There are for example quite a few stories in which people have seen God in some way. Usually these stories are accompanied by the statement: *"Now we must die!"* The story of Samson's parents is an example. They saw the angel of Yahweh, a certain personification of God, and they said, *"We shall surely die, for we have seen God"* (Jg. 13, 22). We also remember from Isaiah his reaction to his vision of Yahweh as the Lord of Lords, the King. He calls out: *"Woe is me, for I am lost"* (Is. 6, 5). There are many other instances, for example in the book of Exodus (33, 18-23) we read that when Moses asked God to show him his glory, God put him into a cleft in a rock until he had passed. Then

Moses was allowed to look briefly, and only at God's back. We also read that when Moses came down from Sinai after speaking with God, his face radiated so much light that he had to cover it with a veil (Exod. 34, 29-35).

The dying which you speak of, what is it? Is it fright or is it a recognition of such grandeur that one, as it were . . .

Yes . . . that a human being, as the bible often says, could not exist or continue to live after seeing God. This presence of God, or rather the revealing of that presence, worked almost as a destroying force. You could compare it to an extremely strong electrical charge, but this is an inadequate comparison. The bible accounts are always given in terms of personal relationships.

The other aspect of God, that he is near, is stressed by the use of anthropomorphisms (speaking about God in human terms). This starts in Paradise, where he is represented as taking clay, giving it the shape of a human being and breathing life into it. Later he is shown closing the door of Noah's ark (Gen. 7, 16). Another example is the attributing of human feelings to God—regrets and joys or, as we have seen in Isaiah, where he was like the dedicated farmer in the vineyard—hope and disappointment.

You said Moses returned from the mountain and his face radiated such a light that he had to cover his face with a veil. Was that an actual fact or was the writer speaking figuratively?

No, that's no metaphor. This came from real experiences in the distant past. But we would need much more time to discuss this extensively. The story as it is known now has the following function in the Israelite tradition: "Mind, you people,

Moses knew God intimately, but don't forget that God is completely different." He associated with God as a friend, *speaking to him face to face* (Exod. 33, 11); that was indeed great intimacy. In spite of this, Moses was allowed to see only God's back for *"My face shall not be seen"* (Exod. 33, 23). So you see there is a constant effort to express these two aspects in stories.

You recall that at the beginning of the book of Job, God is pictured with a whole court of heavenly creatures among whom Satan appears. God asks, in effect, "Satan, what have you been doing on earth lately?" This doesn't strike the Israelite as being disrespectful on the part of the author, and you will have to admit God remains majestic throughout this scene just as he does in Paradise when he shapes the clay and when he breathes life into it, or when he is walking in the garden.

Visible Only in Dedicated People

I still have to give the second part of my answer to your question about God's "bragging." Going home last night I suddenly thought of a text from Jeremiah which perhaps may give a good explanation. You will find it at the beginning of chapter thirteen.

Jeremiah, who lived about a century later than Isaiah, had bought a beautiful linen sash, or belt, which was an indication of his social standing—today people would say it was a "status symbol." But the dear man was not married (He was the great celibate of the Old Testament), and it was a little messy at his place. He had a closet rather full of junk. If you can't understand what bachelor quarters are like, come see my room. He had put his new sash in the closet. It was a very humid house. Some time later when he wanted to wear his sash again, he found it decayed and no longer good for anything. Suddenly that sash became for him a symbol of the people who disappointed God in his expectations of them. Then he says the following in God's name, *"As the sash is attached to somebody's waist, so had I wanted to attach all of the house of Israel and all of the house of Judah to me, says Yahweh, to be my people, my fame, my glory, and my honor. But they did not listen."* Remember that these words were spoken in the awareness that, as we said before, the divine majesty of God can only be manifested on earth through "persons" totally dedicated to him. This is the only way, so to speak, for God to reveal himself in our human world. In this manner something comes to be in our world that we might call an image or even a likeness of God. In the Old Testament Israel has sometimes been named "Servant of Yahweh." A true servant lives only for his master and is guided by his wishes. Being at the beck and call of the master is his whole essence. Several times Israel is called "Son of Yahweh," as for example in Exodus (4, 22). Through its total dedication to Yahweh, Israel must be an image of the ineffable God in human dimensions. That dedication entails that the Israelites recognize Yahweh alone as God, respect him in his majesty, and at the same time respect each other, for as you already know these two attitudes are very closely connected.

What you just said is almost exactly the same as what you said about the prophet Isaiah. Did all the prophets have that same theme of a disappointed God?

Yes, to a certain extent. Of course each prophet lived in a particular era, when there was some sort of crisis. But the prophet as a representative of Yahweh always called upon the revolting people to be absolutely loyal and faithful to God.

*If the people are faithful to God, is the sash made whole?
Does the vineyard produce a good harvest?*

Yes. In plain language, this means that in such a case justice
and charity reign on earth. God wants those who enter into
a personal relationship with him to be his witnesses through
their lives in communication with him and their fellow men.
They constitute "his fame, his glory, and his honor," witness-
ing to him before other people and calling them to follow. In
the case of Job we are dealing with one person who through
faithfulness (at least in the opening chapters) is a witness
for God by saying, *"The Lord gave, and the Lord has taken
away; blessed be the name of the Lord."* And now you may be
able to accept the situation in which God is proud of Job, as
it were.

Our Descriptions Are Insufficient

"As it were . . ." You know, when we Christians speak
about things concerning our religion, we cannot stress
enough that the divine can never be expressed appropriately
in words. The following holds true for all biblical people and
for all Christians. If a person in a real change of heart has experienced something of God's reality, then he knows at the
same time that his words about it are only stammerings. In
fact all expressions of it—words, sentences and even stories—
always fall short, and thus need to be corrected.

A world atlas may serve as an illustration. It's impossible
to reproduce a sphere exactly on a flat surface. Yet we have
to have world maps for practical purposes. Therefore several
projections are used together. On one page, side by side, we
may have two round maps, each picturing one hemisphere.

On another page the earth's surface is pictured on an oblong map (Mercator projection). Both pages picture the whole world, but with enormous aberrations. They complement and somewhat correct each other. Those maps would not make sense to one who does not know that they are projections in two dimensions of the surface of a sphere. Similarly, a person who does not adhere to the convictions of Israel and the Church finds all those biblical expressions of faith unintelligible and full of contradictions. The faithful know what it is about and therefore accept the defective representations. For practical reasons the inexpressible mystery has to be expressed in our dimensions. We are men together, and as such we must *speak* to praise God, to proclaim him and to be able to pass something on to those who come after us.

Israel's Last Chance

Now we really have to begin with the thirteenth chapter of Luke. Here we see Christ acting as a prophet. In the preceding discussions you may have noticed that a prophet does not mean somebody who only foretells the future, as so many people think. He is first of all the representative of God, one who makes known what God wants of his people here and now. Christ called the Jews of his time to conversion. He did not want to argue with them. The same was true for the question of who were the more guilty, those who had been killed or the other people. He refused to go into "theology." For that can easily be a flight from God's call to conversion. Then the beautiful parable of the fig tree follows:

"A man had a fig tree planted in his vineyard; and he came seeking fruit on it and he found none. And he said to the

vinedresser, 'Lo, these three years I have come seeking fruit on this fig tree, and I find none. Cut it down; why should it use up the ground?' And he answered him, 'Let it alone, sir, this year also, till I dig about it and put on manure. And if it bears fruit next year, well and good; but if not, you can cut it down'" (Lk. 13, 6-9).

Every Jew who heard this knew that the rabbi from Nazareth was referring to the people of Israel as the vineyard and the fig tree. The idea of bearing fruit was also a familiar one: it meant deeds of justice and charity. Jesus meant, "Do not postpone your conversion, for this year is the last chance which the Lord of the vineyard, the God of Israel, will give to the fruitless tree, which is you, his people. My appeal is your last chance!"

At the same time Jesus defines his own task very clearly. His part is that of the servant, the gardener, who asks for postponement of sentence. Jesus is the man who faithfully takes care of the business of his master, the vineyard owner—for him he works—but at the same time he defends the barren tree. *"I shall dig about it."* That's quite a warm job in Palestine. *"I shall put manure around it,"* this was quite a modern method for those days—in the Old Testament it hardly ever occurs. *"I shall do everything I can for it. If the tree then still does not bear any fruit, all right, you may cut it down!"* With this Jesus gives a moving description of the nature of his own mission: to be completely on the side of the people, to do everything possible to convert them, and then to leave the judgment of those who refuse to God. In the sequel to Luke's text you will see many examples of how Christ tried to reach the heart of his people.

You use the words "Jesus" and "Christ." Do you do this for variation?

I'm glad that you asked that. Many Jews at that time were named "Jesus." It is almost the same as Joshua. There must have been other boys in Nazareth with the name Jesus.

Is "Christ" some sort of a family name?

No, it is a title: "the Anointed," a Greek translation of the Hebrew word "Messiah." Do you know what we do when we say "Jesus Christ"? We confess that the man from Nazareth, named Jesus, is the long anticipated Messiah. "Christ" indicates his function, his title, and "Jesus" is his first name. Everybody acquires certain habits in his life, and I probably talk mostly about "Jesus" when I am concerned with the man from Nazareth who is preaching and who wants to do everything in his power. When I talk about his function, his role for the well-being of our human race, his function as the Messiah, then I speak more readily about "Christ." But I am certainly not consistent.

Christ is right in the midst of the Jewish people of that era. But if you remove him from that scene and look at him now, is he still disappointed with the Jewish people or does he speak to the people of today?

The second statement is true. I would prefer not to speculate on what the lack of success during his life means to the Jew of today. It is certain that his call to conversion is meant for us too. His foremost idea about that conversion you can read in the third chapter of Luke where the evangelist has John the Baptist explain what conversion means for different categories of people. Whatever food or clothing you have beyond your needs, you should give to others; money lenders may not ask too much of their clients; soldiers may not loot and must be satisfied with their regulation pay; and so on (see

Lk. 3, 10-14). But Jesus goes deeper and demands that the Jewish leaders give up their pharisaical attitude as well.

But let me save this till next time, and then ask if that "pharisaical attitude" was restricted to that particular group of people in history, or if all of us may have a streak of it; and whether, therefore, the call of Jesus to that particular group was not addressed to us also.

SEVEN:
The Message of Jesus

We saw in St. Luke how urgently Jesus called his people to conversion. He wanted not only deeds of justice and charity as John the Baptist did, but he also penetrated the inner attitude from which such deeds should emerge. Hence his clash with the Pharisees, those spiritual leaders of Israel who meant to establish their rights with God by strictly observing all the commandments. Moreover, the Pharisees were of the opinion that they could exclude those who broke the commandments from communion with God. To Jesus these were horrible pretenses and direct attacks on God's majesty. He revealed that majesty by cordially receiving the repenting sinner.

Against this historical background we continue to read the Gospel of Luke. The Pharisees were incensed because the sinners were treated too leniently by Jesus. The loathsome character of this attitude is sharply criticized by Jesus in the parable of the Prodigal Son (Lk. 15) and the workers in the vineyard (Mt. 20).

The Faith of the Pharisees

Our plan was to explain the bible from the historical background of the texts. The gospels will mean more to us when we try to understand the historical climate of the people to whom Jesus was talking. An important group is the Pharisees. The manner in which they are described in the gospels, and consequently pictured in religious instruction and in sermons, unfortunately has created the impression that the Pharisees were bad people. This definitely is not so. We must picture these religious leaders as people who from their youth tried to do the will of God. For them that will was expressed in the commandments of the law. For example, on the Sabbath one was allowed to walk only 1000 paces. Some kept it at 990 to be safe. Another example: one had to tithe for certain things. Some thought, "I'll pay one ninth to be safe; then I'm sure to be right and I know for certain that I have obeyed God and that I am in good standing with him. Then I have nothing to fear . . ."

What they thought about the future "Kingdom of God" may be expressed in this way. When does a king truly reign? Only when his subjects do what he commands. Otherwise it would not be a true authority. The Pharisees also said: "If we do exactly what God tells us to do, he is reigning over us, and for us his promised kingdom has in a small way begun."

Many other Jews did not take all these laws so seriously. There were the publicans, for instance, who collected taxes for the occupying power. Often they extorted money from their fellow countrymen. You can imagine how tremendously evil this appeared to the Pharisees. Also, for example, there were prostitutes in the cities. In fact, in the north, in Galilee, there were whole areas where hardly any attention was given to the Law of God.

The Pharisees said, "All these people, these sinners, are cast out. They certainly do not belong to the kingdom of God. On the contrary, they retard the coming of God's reign. They do not obey him; thus, he does not govern them. Moreover, their disobedience is contagious. Hence we, the pious, ought to avoid these people as we avoid a disease."

However, the Pharisees knew that they too sinned occasionally. For this reason they performed extra deeds of penance by giving alms, fasting and praying in order to make the balance of God's judgment swing favorably to their side.

Why Jesus Was Emphatic

These attitudes of the Pharisees disturbed Christ very much. For although they gave verbal homage to God, they really treated God as their equal. What does it mean when man says: "Listen, I do this-and-that, and God has to accept me"? It means that man attempts to make God his equal. In this manner he fails to recognize God's majesty, his position above everything, totally different from man.

The other attitude was equally appalling. The Pharisees took it upon themselves to exclude others from God's relationship with Israel. They said: "Those publicans and bad women, those Galileans in the north do not belong to God's people because they do not obey his will." Therefore they judged their fellow men, and that is equally an attack on God's majesty. For God is the only one who can and may judge others.

Christ was confronted constantly with this mistaken attitude. You may have read in Luke, after the parable of the fig tree, the story about the healing on the Sabbath. *"Now he was teaching in one of the synagogues on the Sabbath. And there was a woman who had had a spirit of infirmity for eighteen years; she was bent over and could not fully straighten herself. And when Jesus saw her, he called her and said to her, 'Woman you are freed from your infirmity.' And he laid his hands upon her, and immediately she was made straight, and she praised God. But the ruler of the synagogue, indignant because Jesus had healed on the Sabbath, said to the people, 'There are six days on which work ought to be done; come on those days and be healed, and not on the Sabbath day.' Then the Lord answered him [note the plural!] 'You hypocrites! Does not each of you on the Sabbath day untie his ox or his ass from the manger, and lead it away to water it? And ought not this woman, a daughter of Abraham whom Satan bound for eighteen years, be loosed from this bond on the Sabbath day?'"* (Lk. 13, 10-16)

Jesus' protest here was against the misconception of the Pharisees who believed that the Sabbath, as the day of the Lord, is the day on which man may not do this and may not do that, even works of charity. In Jesus' mind they completely missed the point, for the Sabbath was explicitly meant for the benefit of man. In the scriptures it is said: *"Six days you shall do your work, but on the seventh day you shall rest; that your ox and your ass may have rest, and the son of your bondmaid, and the alien, may be refreshed"* (Exod. 23, 12). Sometimes words like the following are added: "It is also for you to rest, to come to peace and remember you were slaves yourselves in the land of Egypt—and at that time you would have been very glad if you could have had one day in seven to rest!" (cf. Deut. 5, 15).

The commandment to rest one day in seven was a humanitarian rule. If there is one day to be good to other people, then it is certainly the Sabbath! But the Pharisees took prohibitions, such as "this is forbidden" and "that is not allowed," so strictly that they excluded all charity. As we have just seen in Luke, Jesus was not permitted to heal on the Sabbath. Imagine! On the day of that Lord who was known since the Exodus as a savior!

Charity That Threatens

A little further in Luke we see Jesus again speaking as a prophet—namely, in verse 23 and the following. There again the people ask him a theoretical question: "Lord, will those who are saved be few? We would like to discuss the problem with you whether there will be few or many people who finally enter the kingdom of God?" Christ answers: *"Strive to enter by the narrow door!"*

What does he mean by the narrow door?

Well, he indicates that a total dedication, a complete giving and renouncing of oneself, is necessary in order to share in that final salvation. Instead of idling away time discussing theology, try to get to heaven. Here we see Jesus truly speaking as a prophet. Immediately following the parable of the narrow gate is one of the many examples he gives to indicate the urgency of his call. As we have already noted in the parable of the fig tree, the worker asked for a postponement of a year to do everything possible for the tree, but when that year was over, the last chance was lost. This idea of a last chance comes back again and again. Here (in Luke 13, 25-27) it is the master of the house who, at a certain moment, closes the door. The chance to enter is gone. You are outside. You may knock and say: "Lord, we have been with you!" That does not help. The door is closed. Jesus continually expresses such warnings.

Then follows one of the rare occasions when Christ explicitly mentions the heathen. Note that he warns with a serious threat, "If you do not accept salvation, which was meant for you in the first place, all right; then God will reject you and he will draw to him all those heathen people whom you despise!" (cf. 13, 28-29)

The heathen are also mentioned in the parable of the un-willing wedding guests, in the next chapter of Luke (14, 16-24). You recall that some of those who were invited had excuses. One had bought a piece of land, another—five yoke of oxen, and a third had just married. Then the lord of the feast commands his servant to go into the street and bring the poor, the needy, the blind and the crippled into the banquet hall. Here Jesus probably means the publicans and sinners within Israel. When it appears there is still more room, the lord of the feast sends his servants to the roads and the squares outside the city to gather guests. "City" clearly means the Jewish community. The "lord" is God who upon refusal from the Jewish leaders reacts by bringing the pagans into the salvation that was intended for Israel. Therefore this parable ends in an ominous threat. *"I say unto you not one of the people that were invited will enjoy my banquet!"*

Jesus—An "Insider" with God

There are people who say that Jesus, with all his warnings and appeals, was only playing a game. Being God, didn't he know beforehand whether or not the Jews would be converted?

Those people should first listen to what we said about the impossibility of speaking correctly about God. Then they would realize how wrong their reasoning is. Their point of departure is the creed or the catechism which says: "Jesus is God." Then they make the mistake of using the term "God" as if they know exactly what it means. They imagine him to be some sort of superman who knows everything and can do everything. Consequently, Jesus must be all-knowing and om-nipotent. What, then, do they mean when they confess to " 'the

Incarnation' of the Son of God?" He became a concrete human being, a specific man of the particular Jewish people of that time. As such, he was subject to all the limitations of knowledge that people possessed at that time. For example, he did not know that the earth was round. He could not speak Latin, unless perhaps a few words. The only area in which he was a perfect specialist—if I may use that word—was in the things of God, that is to say in the relation of God to man and what the attitude of man toward God ought to be. Jesus came to proclaim this ("the Kingdom of God"), and what's more, to realize it—to bring it about by himself in a manner which is mysterious and beyond our comprehension.

If he knew only the relationship between man and God, doesn't this mean he is not God? How can we say he was truly God?

Remember what we discussed about the impossibility of expressing anything concerning God in exact words. Then you may understand that your remark belongs among the most difficult ones that you could bring up. You can't expect to grasp offhand answers to questions which demand so much thought.

Nevertheless let me try to say in simple words what we can derive from the gospels. Jesus lived, so to speak, in a continuous communication with God the Father, of whom he always speaks in such a special manner. He often speaks about "my Father" and also of "your Father," but he never includes himself with people in one group saying, "our Father." He wants us to pray "our Father" as one large human family. He himself clearly lives in a unique intimate relationship with the Father. As Matthew says: *"All things have been delivered to me by the Father; and no one knows the Son except the Father, and no one knows the Father except the Son"* (11, 27). He does not say, "I am the Son," but speaks about the Son in the third person. Yet it is clear that he means himself. His "speciality" consists apparently in that unique relationship with God. He talks about God with a remarkable ease as if he were an "insider" with God. But somewhere else he says: *"But of that day or that hour no one knows, not even the angels in heaven, nor the Son, but only the Father"* (Mk. 13, 32). So if we say "He is God," we're speaking of a personal and unique relationship with God which is characteristic and essential in Jesus. So it's good that we read the gospels and learn to see God through him.

To put it another way, we shouldn't start with the catechism truth that "Jesus is God" and think to ourselves: "We know what God is; hence Jesus has to be like that; he has to act this or that way." The purpose of his coming into this world is just the other way around. We *don't* know what God is, and that is what he comes to show us. We can learn how God approaches us from the manner in which Jesus approaches people.

You may recall what we discussed last time: God can only become visible on this earth in a group of people or in one human who is completely dedicated to him. Such a person may be called his "servant" or even his "son," a human image of the Invisible. Jesus was totally dedicated to God, and therefore he was God's image. He expressed this repeatedly by saying that he always fulfilled the will of his heavenly Father. Hence every reaction to his fellow man, each word he spoke, was really God's reaction to man, God speaking to man. Here we have before us concretely, translated into a human life, the manner in which he, who is our Creator, our beginning and our end, approaches us. Herein lies the unique value of the gospels.

This has to be stated clearly, and it cannot be repeated often enough. When, for example, a sinner comes to Christ and says,

"I was wrong and I want to begin anew," he is immediately accepted. This means that everyone in the world who honestly turns to God can be assured of immediate acceptance by God.

The All-Forgiving Father

If you read further in the Gospel of St. Luke, you have met the story of the Prodigal Son in chapter fifteen. The story, or parable, ought to be entitled: "The Parable of the All-Forgiving Father." The story has such grandeur that we can't appreciate it here. It should be read in an appropriate atmosphere. But let me now point out some of its details. While living among people of the Mideast, I often noted the fact that walking slowly indicates a man's dignity. A prominent man should never walk fast. In the parable, Jesus relates that this father —he is wealthy and prominent without a doubt—is waiting, and when he sees his son returning he runs to meet him. He runs! He forgets all conventional rules. The son has learned a little speech by heart to address his father: *"Father, I have sinned against heaven and before you; I am no longer worthy to be called your son; treat me as one of your hired servants."* But the father does not give him a chance to finish his little speech. He interrupts him and says to the servant: *"Bring quickly the best robe . . . and bring the fatted calf and kill it."*

Note that the eldest son, who cannot bear the fact that his brother was accepted even before he expressed his repentance, remains outside, sulking. The father goes to him and pleads, "Please, come inside and join in the joy of the feast." It is very striking how bitterly and harshly the son answers. In spite of this, his father calls him affectionately, "My son."

The sulking son represents the Pharisees. They have always said: "A sinner may want to be converted, but he first will have to make amends, and then he must do a great deal of penance. For this he needs many, many years and most probably he will not make it before his death." Then Jesus of Nazareth proclaims that a remorseful sinner no longer has to make amends. Imagine! We do our best all our lives for the kingdom of God, and now Jesus casually states that people who sinned for many years without a worry can get into the kingdom, just like that!

Jesus does not tell how the story ends, and that's very considerate of him. He leaves it to the imagination of his listeners, the Pharisees, to think up the ending—whether the elder son stuck to his refusal or whether he finally gave in and joined in the feast. Jesus actually says to the Pharisees, "This is your attitude, you are the sulking son, but you can change your ways; you can still rejoice in the message of divine mercy that I announce!"

He is less considerate in the parable of the workers of the eleventh hour (Mt. 20, 1-15). Those who worked long are angry because the lord gives them the same wages as those who came late and did practically nothing. They are angry because he is so good.

We must always be grateful for the fact that Jesus does the Father's will in every word and gesture, and that he, in so doing, shows to every man how his God approaches him. Think how the fifteenth chapter of Luke begins—the Pharisees reproach Jesus for inviting sinners and mixing with them. He answers in parables which show how gladly and joyfully God receives sinners. In other words, Jesus justifies his own behavior by pointing to the behavior of God! By noting such details, we shall be able to grasp the real meaning of Jesus as "truly" God—"God with us."

EIGHT:
How the Gospels Were Written

We have tried to learn and understand the meaning of Christ as "God-with-us" from his way of life in our midst. We used a number of Gospel texts without asking to what extent they give an accurate historical account of events. We will take up this question now. Again we use a diagram, this time dealing with the first century of the Christian calendar. It shows that Paul had already died when the oldest Gospel, that of Mark, was written. Then the Gospels of Matthew and Luke follow, incorporating portions of Mark. Finally, later than the three "synoptic gospels," we see the very different Gospel of St. John. Thus it appears that the memories of what Jesus said and did went through a long history before those four authors gave them definitive form. The richness of these four small books consists partly in the fact that they reflect the way of life of the first Christians, their preaching, their instruction, their discussions with the Jews and their liturgical celebrations. But most important they presented Jesus as he really was.

When we talked about the Old Testament in earlier discussions, we often saw that its authors had a very strong awareness of the divine mystery. God is inexpressible. He cannot be "comprehended" in any form. Yet at the same time God is inconceivably close to us. We cannot speak about him without his listening. Actually we cannot even speak if he does not make us speak. The people of the bible realized this; *"In him we live and move and have our being"* (Acts 17, 28). So if we try to consider God as outsiders, we are no longer talking about him. With God nobody is an outsider. Such is the mystery which we call "God."

Israel's God Visible in Jesus

In line with our last discussion I wonder if we can observe something similar in Jesus of Nazareth—the same paradox of distance and closeness. He is very close to all people and mixes with everybody, in particular with the simple ordinary people and the outcasts who "labor and are heavy laden" (Mt. 12, 28). He is subject to all human sentiments: joy, sorrow, disappointment. And in particular he knows pain and suffering from experience; and these are among the most essential characteristics of human existence.

But at the same time he appears to be completely apart from people. We noticed that difference in the way he points to God as *"your* Father . . ." and *"my* Father . . ." Apparently he lives in a different relationship with God than do his fellow men. In all his modesty he is conspicuously authoritative and claims to supersede the authority of Moses. This must have sounded like blasphemy in the ears of his Jewish listeners.

That he is indeed very different from us is made particularly clear by his suffering. He drinks the dregs of the chalice of suffering and remains composed and in control of himself and the situation. Imagine! On his way to the cross people come to show him their pity. The only thing he thinks of is the fact that those people are soon to suffer themselves, and he pities their pain. In his agony on the cross he can bring himself to pay attention to the man who is suffering next to him. He is tremendously free and disengaged from all attention to himself. He does not seem to have an "ego" in the sense of a center which pulls everything toward itself. Perhaps this is the reason why God's love for us can flow freely through him, can express itself completely in him, so that he can put into effect what "God-with-us" means.

You always talk about the gospels as if they were merely historical accounts. I thought modern biblical scholarship strongly denies that fact. Could you go into it more fully? I think others are troubled by it too.

Yes, surely. However this will require some exertion on the part of the audience. We shall be obliged to take the four gospels quite seriously as a special form of literature, as four booklets written by special people under special circumstances with special purposes. We have to go back into history, and this is usually more difficult and less appealing than impressive general statements. And we have to resort to another diagram of dates.

Please recall first our discussion about the way the Israelites lived their faith through the ages. I don't remember whether or not we discussed the conviction which influenced Israel's faith more and more. The Israelites came to believe that Yahweh directs history's course to a goal, a goal which must be his glorification—the revealing of the fact that he is Lord. To say it differently, Israel lived in the expectation of "the kingdom of God," or rather, a time of final fulfillment when God alone would reign. It meant that men would obey him. Suffering and death would be eliminated, for they are attendant signs of man's break with the living God. People expected this and knew that God was always working to prepare it. During the time of Christ, Palestine was occupied by the Romans. The misgovernment of the Herodian kings and the Roman land-lords weighed very heavily on the Jews. Therefore the desire for the royal reign of Israel's God was very strong. The people desperately longed for the moment when God (and his people!) would again take the situation in hand. There were all sorts of nationalistic movements which the Jews practically indentified with "Messianic" movements. One of these was that of John the Baptist, which was more spiritual than patriotic in nature. Jesus broke with his group. For three years more or less—we don't know exactly how long—he proclaimed the imminent coming of the kingdom of God. This took but a short period of his own life and only a tiny fraction of history. He was like a meteor flashing through history. Yet he changed the lives of multitudes of people, and continues to do so.

The Result of an Explosion

Although it is not a very valid comparison, I sometimes compare the effect of Jesus and his teaching with the explosion of an atomic bomb. There is a tremendous flash of light, so sudden and blinding that nobody can really see it. It cannot be photographed. All we can know is the result: a city is in ruins, homes are destroyed, and, most tragically, thousands of lives are snuffed out or changed forever by that one flash. In a similar way Jesus appeared on the human scene—a very sudden "event" which had tremendous influence on the lives of men for all succeeding generations.

The significant date of Christian history corresponds to the beginning of Jesus' ministry. After Jesus died on the cross, his disciples and then more and more people came under the influence of that event. They began a totally new life. When they were thus "converted," they suddenly found a new perspective. In surrender to Jesus as their Lord and Master, their God, they were aware for the first time of their responsibilities toward every other human being. They were impelled to active witness; they hoped for and they expected the speedy fulfillment of what God began in Christ. This was the case with the disciples whom Jesus called to be with him. The circle quickly expanded. St. Paul's first missionary journey covered roughly the years 43 to 49 when he brought to Asia Minor the joyous tidings of God's coming in Christ. The other apostles did the same thing in other areas, but we know almost nothing about their missionary endeavors. It happens that we know only about Paul's work.

The council of Jerusalem, held about the year 50, was followed shortly by the second journey of Paul. He crossed to Europe and arrived in the big harbor city of Thessalonica, the present-day Salonika, then went to Athens and Corinth. During this journey, in about the year 51, he wrote his first letter to the Thessalonians, which thus stands as the oldest written part of the New Testament. The letter is an incidental writing occasioned by the news of the newly converted faithful at Thessalonica. He could not go there immediately, and so he thought, "I shall write these people a letter." How little did he suspect that this letter was to become part of the bible! The third missionary journey lasted from about 53 to 58. Paul visited Asia Minor and Greece again, and during that time he wrote the so-called long letters, such as those to the Romans, the Galatians, and the Corinthians. Finally he landed in prison in Rome where he was confined from about the years 60 to 62, and here he wrote several other letters. He died about the year 64 or a little later.

These letters bear witness to the first Christian generation—those for whom the Christ-event was a matter of personal experience. Most of the other apostolic letters could be added to complete this list. The year 70 marked the fatal date in Jewish history: the destruction of Jerusalem by the Romans. The temple, which for the Jews was the only residence of God among men, was destroyed.

Oral Tradition

We can place the gospels within the framework of this history. In the short time of his public life, Jesus taught and imprinted in the minds of his disciples all sorts of sayings and parables, and he performed many miracles. His legacy was his words and his deeds. The memories of these were kept and passed on to the new converts in answer to their questions about Christ. How is it, they asked, that this Jesus whom they recognized as Lord and Messiah was not recognized by the Jews to whom he addressed himself? The discussion that Jesus had with the Pharisees, for example, might comprise an answer to that question. More questions were asked: "What did he really say about charity, which he called the greatest commandment?" "How did he picture the kingdom of God?" And then again his teachings and parables and short statements were related, as well as a number of stories about his deeds, healings, exorcisms and so on. All this was passed on by word of mouth to the communities that were formed everywhere. The catechist or teacher would relate, for example, a number of disputes with the Pharisees one after another in such a way that a line ran through them, building to a climax. In this way the narrations received a definitive form. If you have experienced something and have to narrate it frequently, then it's quite normal for you to relate certain points of your story in the same way. Little by little it takes on a definitive form.

So the tidings which Paul announced were handed down only by word of mouth? He could not yet use the written word?

No, not the written word. However he could use the source that existed, the stories that others had passed on orally. St. Paul himself was very close to this "tradition." He himself did not belong to the first group of disciples, but after his conversion he stayed in close contact with them. On his second journey he was very happy to have Silas (Silvanus) as a companion, one of the most highly placed persons of the Church in Jerusalem, who knew everything at first hand.

In the fast-growing Christian communities in Palestine and elsewhere, a disciple of Christ might ask someone for help with his instructions and sermons. He could write down some things, especially the stories which he always related. That's probably how written summaries of Jesus's words and stories about him were prepared by the disciples and came to be used.

The First Written Reports

Let's say that about the year 50 such written synopses of Jesus' words and deeds existed. They were used and passed on to other catechists and to the faithful. But oral tradition was still the main method and would remain so for the time being. Before the year 70 one synopsis was written. It was an organized entity of recollections of Jesus's deeds which came to be called the "Gospel according to Saint Mark." The writer begins the account with the public appearance of John the Baptist and ends it with the appearances of Jesus after his death.

Did Mark know that it would become "bible" or did he just write?

Good question. We should realize that until the year 100 all these Christians, including Paul, knew and used a "bible," the book we call the Old Testament. They had no idea what they wrote would ever become part of the bible as we know it.

Did Mark perhaps want to make a sort of supplement to the Bible?

No, this probably wasn't his intention. It's more likely that he thought along this line: "Let me put a number of these stories about Jesus together in a short booklet, or brochure." Such a description of Jesus' public life, his death on the cross and his resurrection was really *the* Gospel, *the* joyous tidings. The narration of the life of Jesus of Nazareth, the way he lived and died, how he rose from the dead—this sequence of facts means that God has come so near to man with his love and mercy that now there is a prospective, a hope and future for everyone who turns to Jesus.

Then they must have believed that Jesus was God.

Yes, indeed, they believed that in him God came in person to us. "To be converted" meant explicitly to accept Jesus as absolute Lord and Master over oneself—to recognize him as God.

Wasn't the Gospel of Mark the written replica of the preachings of Peter?

Yes, the old Christian tradition calls him the "interpreter of Peter." But he must also have had other sources, as appears from an analysis of his Gospel. But first let's go a bit further. About the year 80, roughly ten years after the composition of

Mark's Gospel, the longer Gospel according to Matthew appeared. It is easy to show that the author who wrote it used the Gospel of Mark as a source. He worked it into his gospel, but used other sources as well. This evangelist captured, as it were, still other rays from the resplendent stream of tradition and put his gospel in the line of that of Mark, but with much more material.

The Synoptic Gospels

Why did Matthew want to write his gospel?

Before I answer this perhaps we might examine the situation at the time. You realize that communities and churches soon came into being, first in Jerusalem, then all over Palestine, and then further and further away. Many of these communities, such as for example that in Antioch, wanted to have the stories of Jesus' words and deeds all together for the instruction of new members and younger Christians. Some people tried to synthesize all the stories. There were certainly many who did this, but in the end only four of those booklets have survived. One is Mark, the second is Matthew with its own characteristics, and the third, Luke, somewhat longer than the first two.

About the year 1200 the bible books were divided into chapters (by an English bishop, Stephan Langton) and in the 16th century these chapters were again divided into sentences which were numbered and called "verses," strangely enough. Since that time we say chapter so-and-so and verse such-and-such.

Mark has 661 verses, Matthew 1,076, which is quite a bit more, and Luke is longer still with 1,150 verses. Luke, too, used the Gospel of Mark, and other sources as well. Still lower on our diagram comes the Gospel of John. This reached its definite shape well after the year 80 and is shorter than Matthew and Luke, with 879 verses. This evangelist also drew from the wealth of stories that had been passed on orally, but he used them in a manner entirely his own. That's why his gospel stands somewhat apart from the synoptical gospels.

What does it actually mean, the word "synoptic"?

This means that you can see them together (*syn*) at one glance (*opsis*). If you print them in columns next to each other you noticed that they are often very similar, and sometimes exactly the same. Hence we have many of Jesus' talks and descriptions of his deeds in three different versions, sometimes agreeing and sometimes quite different from each other. In almost every part of any Gospel—Mark, Matthew, or Luke—you will be concerned with three things: First, with a word or deed of Jesus, and second with the manner in which the contents were passed on by the disciples. For instance your explanation to an adult will differ from the explanation to a child; your audience influences your performance. Thus the form of what was passed on is determined somewhat by the audience—the first faithful. In the third place you are dealing with the evangelist, the man who said, "Now I am going to put all of this together in a gospel. I shall choose from Mark or some other already written synthesis or from that which is circulating among the people. I shall put it together in such a way as to stress certain things for those who will read my gospel." Hence each evangelist puts his personal stamp on his gospel. If you read Mark's gospel without interruption you will notice how strongly he stresses the mystery of Jesus' person; he is the Son of God who can at will dispose of God's powers. A deep mystery seems to confront us: the Gospel is filled with the premonition that this divine person has to suffer.

Matthew's gospel reflects the instruction in a Christian community, and probably originates from a group of catechists. Many of Jesus' words are formulated and put together in such a manner that the people can find a guideline in it for Christian behavior. (Think of the sermon on the mount.) For this reason much in our Sunday Missal is taken from Matthew.

Luke was a historian, the only gentile among the evangelists, a convert from paganism. For Theophilus, an educated friend of his, he wrote a description of the "history of salvation" in two parts. First he related the life of Jesus from the very beginning, and then in the Acts of Apostles he told of the life of the Church, also from the very beginning on Pentecost.

A Special Kind of Historical Writing

By this time you probably realize that the question of the extent to which the Gospels can be considered "historical documents" can be answered only with certain reservations. It is clear that those works recall many of the impressions that Jesus made on his fellow men, especially on his intimate friends, and hence are personal memories of his way of life and his words. *At the same time* they reflect the manner in which he lived on among them, and how he kept on influencing them and all the others who accepted the story about his life, death and resurrection as God's message.

If you want to know what kind of a person or historical figure he really was, you must not overlook his influence on the people around him. For this reason the letters of the apostles belong to the documents which help us understand who Jesus really was. When Paul writes, *"For me to live is Christ, and to die is gain,"* because he can then be *"with Christ"* forever and undisturbed (Phil. 1, 21 and 23), he tells us something about Jesus as he actually was, namely, that long after his death he was able to give meaning to one's entire human life.

Can we say then that the Gospels are historical, but in a different sense from regular historical descriptions?

If we limit "historical" to a purely statistical report of facts which can be registered with precise dates and hours, places and outward circumstances, then we can hardly call the gospels historical. But history is no longer defined in such a way by the most prominent people in the field. Historians now pay more attention to the things that really mattered in the lives of important people. Along with the purely factual things which these people did, the authors describe the intentions and motives that were behind the actions—also how they were influenced by their environment and how their environment in turn was influenced by them. The latter is especially important. For it is exactly because of that influence that they became great men in history, that they "made history." If you take "historical description" in this sense, then the gospels are extremely "historical," and the other writings of the New Testament also present all kinds of details which give us a picture of Jesus as he really was.

NINE:
Understanding the Gospels

There are four gospels. In spite of the fact that one had already been written, three other evangelists began to write theirs. Why did they do this? And here is another question: We have always been taught that those books were written under the inspiration of the Holy Spirit. What does this mean?

It certainly doesn't mean that it's easy for the average reader to understand these books in detail. The message of the gospels is simple, though difficult to put into practice; the texts themselves require interest and attention on the part of the reader who wants to analyze them for their real meaning. Not everyone is expected to put forth this effort. However, this is necessary for Catholics who consider themselves well informed, particularly when they discuss Christianity and the Church, and more so if they have to instruct or teach. We shall discuss this further with the help of a diagram of the historical facts that preceded the gospels. This will show that these books present us with a historical account of exceptional credibility.

Why Four Gospels and Not One?

My question is: why four evangelists? I mean, if I want to

*write on a particular subject and I know that someone else
has already written on it, then I am not going to repeat it.*

Evidently you're not a professional writer. If everybody
did what you suggest and wrote only on a subject that no one
else had written about, then book stores would soon be out of
business.

*But if a well-known author has written about a subject, that
ought to be sufficient.*

Try to imagine two things. First, it was not long before the
orally-transmitted stories about Jesus were collected and organized in a certain order. Mark recorded this information in
a larger unit for a certain group of people. We don't know for
which group or where, but it was first intended for local use.
Second, this "gospel," originally meant for a special group of
people, was then spread to others. Book printing had not yet
been invented, but there were so-called scriptoria or "copy
shops" at that time. They served the same purpose as our printing shops do today. One gave them a manuscript and asked for
so many copies. A reader read the document aloud and the
copiers did the writing. But that was rather expensive for the
Christians who were generally poor people, and so they probably did their own copy work. At any rate, the Gospel of
Mark began to circulate and was passed on to others. And so
that little book also came to be known in the community
where the Gospel according to Matthew was to originate. Besides Mark's Gospel, other sources were also available, oral as
well as written. Then a teacher wrote a booklet much like
Mark's story but more extensive and didactic. It contained
additional information on the teachings of Jesus.

Were there more than four evangelists?

Yes, but only these four gospels have remained. The other written sources which they used have disappeared, and other attempts at complete "gospels" apparently didn't succeed. What makes a book a success? It has something to tell people, something important which is recognized as such at the time and by succeeding generations. The book that sells well is printed over and over again and becomes a "classic." If this does not happen to a book, it disappears from the market, although at present practically every publication is kept in a library. The other gospels (a few of which are still known to us, but written after our four Gospels) were not accepted by the Church.

Was there a deliberate choice to limit the number of gospels to four, or was the number purely accidental?

The Church continued using four alone, saying, "Everything is here." Later on some thought the number four worthy of note. For biblical people it was full of symbolism. It pointed to a totality, an all-embracing entity—such as the four winds and the four mysterious creatures in Ezekiel's vision. But from our human point of view, the number was accidental, if you wish.

Our Obligation To Read Them

Let me ask a more practical question. Is it necessary that a Christian read all four gospels, or may he limit himself to one?

That all depends on his wishes, disposition and character.

However—and I am going to repeat again what I stated before—you can be a perfectly good and holy Christian without ever reading the scriptures. If you love God and your neighbor, and if you go to Church on Sunday in order to meet God in Christ there together with others, and if you are again encouraged to try to make that charity into something real, then you are reassured that your efforts will one day be rewarded. That's sufficient for everybody.

But if you have a position of leadership in the Christian community, or if you are a person who tries to be a thinking individual, someone who reads a great deal, or if you want to have a responsible explanation for your Christian faith or explain it to others, then you are of course obliged to read the bible often in order to know it. Read particularly the gospels, for these are the first records of the effects of that "explosion" with which we compared Jesus' appearance and which is still active. They are, so to speak, our "classics." If you read them as a modern person, thinking along the lines of history, then you will be confronted with questions. For instance: when I read in Luke of the parable of the wedding banquet, with all those guests who had excuses, and the same in Matthew, where the narration is quite different, I wonder, "How is that possible? What did Jesus actually say?"

Yes, but I still don't think that it's very important to know all this.

No, it is certainly not necessary. For, as we said before, you may open the bible at random in a reverent attitude, in a spirit of prayer, and let the word itself speak to you without further commentary. Nevertheless, if you have a guiding and instructing role in the Christian community, however modest it may be, the necessity becomes evident. I compare this at times with something with which I have had no experience (at least up to now!). I suppose one could be a good communist by knowing a few very simple principles and by putting himself at the service of the movement in the spirit of those principles. However, if he has a leading function, then he ought to know the classical literature of the movement—for example, the works of Marx and Stalin. He has to know the history of communism, how the doctrine and its application developed; he should know a little about the speeches and books of Mao and the present relations in world communism. Otherwise he cannot properly fulfill his function as a leader. Superficial activities and repetitions of slogans are not sufficient.

In the movement which we call the Church, the same seems to be true. The Christian who must exercise leadership or who wants to discuss Christianity or the Church responsibly must know the bible. If his knowledge is limited to the catechism, a few dogmas and laws, he cannot expect to lead with conviction, nor will his opinions be of much value.

Not for Everybody

That's the reason for the question mark after the title of the first chapter ("The Bible for Every Man?"). A person who grew up in a family where the bible was used daily can later in life easily be touched by a text from the bible without having to search for the original meaning and the historical background. But such an education is a rare privilege.

Other people have to begin to read the bible just as you read other books from the past, by considering what the author's intention was in that particular historical situation, what forms of expression his environment had to offer, and so on. This requires a certain level of education, but above all it demands interest and attention. Not everybody can meet these conditions.

I have often thought of comparing the bible with secular literature. The works of literary authors are not comprehended by everyone either.

Yes, that seems to be right, but there is one difference. What is described in the gospels—namely "the" Gospel, the Good News—is really addressed to everyone. But if reading those four books were the only way to receive that message, to come to an understanding of it and to put it into practice, then we would be in bad shape.

We say we know the message of the bible through tradition and the teaching of the Church. Actually it's simple to formulate: "Love God and your neighbor"—although it's not so simple to put into practice. We also know from the gospels that Christ remains with us. For instance, he said we would better understand his words as time went on, through the power of the Spirit he would send. Our situation in trying to understand Christ's words, then, seems to be quite different from trying to figure out the meaning of a poet who lived a hundred years ago, and whose purpose in writing is difficult to know.

Exactly! And Christ's Spirit can make use of the preachers of the Church. Let me illustrate again by means of the story of Jonah. You recall that the book of Jonah reveals the message of God's love for all people. It is also a satire about the Jews who mistakenly thought God's interest was limited to their tribe and who therefore were waiting for the destruction of other nations. As we said before, if you read this booklet, this short story, to people in church without explanation, they may wonder, "What a big fish with such a small throat! How is it possible; how can a person live so long in the stomach of a fish?" But if you give a brief introduction, saying, "Friends, this story contains a certain message," then they will pay attention to the main things, and the message will be understood better.

It is exactly the same with the gospels. Sometimes I give my sermon before I read the Gospel, by way of introduction and explanation, thus ending with an essential reading to which nothing needs to be added. This seems to me to be better. At any rate, the most important words are the words of the bible itself. Everything I've told you in these discussions is really a kind of general introduction. We really ought to have the opportunity to come together more often and read a passage of the bible in light of the background acquired in these discussions. Then we could make a comparative study of the four gospels to see how each writer approached the Christ-event, how he understood the message and finally put his information into words.

A Dutch psychologist once wrote a book about the four evangelists as "human types." According to him, they represent four different types of human temperament. This is remarkable, for in the gospels we see Jesus through the eyes of four different types of people.

The Fourth Gospel

You said that Luke, Mark and Matthew each wrote for a certain group of people. If I remember correctly, you remarked in an earlier discussion that John wrote with a different motive.

No, not really. John wrote for a particular audience also, although he was most likely thinking of the whole Church of the future. It seems that this evangelist didn't have the other three Gospels before him but drew from the stories that had been handed down by word of mouth and used them in a very special and personal manner. This gospel pictures Jesus in his meaning for the second and third generation of Christians, and thus for all generations. It's a great book. You can read it over and over again. Father Lagrange, the founder of the Dominican Bible School in Jerusalem, had to return to France in his later years because of ill health. He still taught the young Dominicans a few classes on the book of Genesis and on the Gospel of St. John. At that time he was supposed to have said something along this line: "If heaven were nothing more than being allowed to read and to reflect and meditate quietly on this gospel, then I should be more than happy." In the so-called "farewell speech" in St. John's Gospel (chapters 13-17) we learn what Jesus wanted to be for us even now, and what his innermost motives were, in terms which can touch every human being personally. We might actually say that the fourth Gospel teaches us how to understand the Christ pictured in the other three.

We must be on our guard and not lose sight of the real message by spending too much time in comparing texts.

We must read the bible in such a way as to do the one without neglecting the other. On the one hand, we ought to study a section with the aid of some expert who explains its details and background. Articles in journals commenting on the gospels can be clarifying—fortunately such articles are becoming more and more available all the time. We should take a good look at such a gospel text, compare the parallel texts, examine the differences and try to arrive at the original statements of Jesus. On the other hand, we ought to hear that same text read to us sometime in Church. There it touches us differently and clearly fulfills its true purpose: to deliver a message to us. I think that both ways of listening to the bible can influence each other favorably. So we should use both methods.

"Inspired" Writing

What do you mean when you say the gospels were written under inspiration of the Holy Spirit?

That's very difficult. Let me point out that Jesus and the apostles and all Jews of their time considered the scriptures (that is, the Old Testament) to be the work of prophets and authors through whom God spoke to his people. His "spirit" (which is the same as "breath") had breathed, as it were, the words into them. This is the meaning of "in-spired." The same 'Spirit of Yahweh" worked powerfully in Jesus and was, after his glorification, "poured forth" on his disciples. In the second century, the writings of the first disciples which began to circulate were also considered to be "books inspired by the Spirit." They were added to the known bible, and in this manner the complete book, consisting of the Old and New Testaments, came into being.

Expressions such as "inspired by the Holy Spirit," "inspiration," and also the "word of God" are therefore very old. All of them attempt to illustrate the special character of the only book that goes back to the historic roots of our religious existence. The bible gives a direct account of Israel's way of life in association with God and of the disciples' way of life in their association with Jesus.

I'd like to know if people could still verify these stories about Jesus when, for example, Luke was writing. The people

*who saw Jesus had to be eighty years old at least. Or is that
an odd question?*

No, indeed, that's a good question. If I remember correctly,
we began to talk about how the gospels were written last time
because of doubts on this subject. Let me just add something
about the stories of Jesus' words and deeds.

He instructed his disciples well; he followed the Jewish
method, using terse sentences and usually very short similes
and parables. We saw this in Isaiah. You are not going to
forget a parable like the one of the vineyard, particularly not
the end with its short, rhyming words. Unfortunately we
have Jesus' words only in a Greek translation. But a few words
can be easily translated back into the Aramaic language that
he spoke, and then it's quite noticeable how strong the language was, how striking, often with alliteration and rhyme.
He also used very touching metaphors, often poignant and
incisive, so that one could not forget them after hearing them
once. Therefore it's likely that many of those words
were handed down verbatim, and that their translation into
Greek could hardly fail to be accurate. The first Christian
communities in Palestine were bilingual. Words of Jesus recorded in Greek could be checked by people who knew the
Aramaic form of those phrases. You may compare Jerusalem
of that era to Brussels—also a bilingual city. There, if you
should render a certain phrase incorrectly in French, there are
enough people who know both French and Flemish so fluently
that they could say, "You are not saying that correctly." For
this reason, a great many of Jesus' words in the gospels have
been handed down faithfully. You can also be sure that many
parables, such as the Prodigal Son, are recorded exactly as Jesus
told them.

As for his deeds, people remembered the many times that
he cast out devils and healed the sick. This was part of his

message—that the kingdom of God was near and already actively at work in him. Where God's reign is established, Satan's domain is restricted; sickness and death will no longer be found there. These miracles were a part of his proclamation, they indicated the purpose of his coming, they pointed toward deeper hidden things. Later, when the story of how he cured a blind person, for example, was passed on, the Christians were interested mainly in the meaning of the story. What he did then, he still does in a deeper sense for us. He also cured us from blindness. At one time we were in the dark, wondering where we were going and what the sense of our existence was. Then we accepted the Gospel and he cured us of that blindness. In the story about the five thousand being fed with five loaves and two fishes, the Christians heard above all what they themselves experienced each time they celebrated the eucharist: the distribution time and again of the same wondrous bread.

That's why you discover in the Gospel that some of the details which were handed down are related differently. The first reason for this is that these stories were written by different people for different groups. The second and main reason is the fact that the *meaning* of the miracles played such an important role. We in the modern world are interested in exact facts—what, when, why—an interest that did not exist among the Jews at all. We should consider this if we want to read the Gospel stories critically, in the good sense of the word.

In one of Father Lagrange's books about the gospels he uses a Greek proverb as a motto: "A hidden harmony is better than an obvious one." If the four gospels would concur in details, then you might think the four authors came to an agreement to make them all the same. However, it is exactly because of all those differences that the gospels are so historically reliable. Basically the same person is projected, but as experienced by different people. And this is what makes the gospels so tremendously rich.

But isn't John's approach different? I'm thinking of Christ's farewell speech, for example.

Yes, the fourth gospel reflects an exceptionally high degree of spiritual assimilation and growth which occurred in the years between the disciples' historical contact with Jesus and the formulation of this gospel. This spiritual "living on" in faith after Christ's glorification includes the relationship of the faithful disciple with his Lord, or what Christ now means for a person who believes in him. The evangelist puts words into Jesus' mouth, explaining the deepest meaning of his life and death, words which Jesus could not have spoken while he lived on this earth.

Would you give an example of this?

Yes, there are many. For example, there is the statement: "Before Abraham was, I am" (Jn. 8, 58). This expresses Jesus' mission and divinity very deeply, a statement that he could not have made during his life on earth.

Why not?

Let's talk about that next time.

TEN:
The Words of Jesus

The events recorded in the gospels took place in an order which was the reverse of the way it is presented. Jesus had always talked about God and man's attitude toward God, and he tried to divert any attention directed toward himself. After his resurrection this changed completely; the disciples now spoke in particular about *him*. First they bore witness to his rising from the dead, then they relived their memories of what he had said and done during his "public life." Later on, recollections about Jesus as a person took the shape of stories about his origin. The awareness that he lived among them as their Lord gave those first disciples a freedom in their descriptions of Jesus' life which surprises us. It takes some effort to understand the way in which all this came about. Likewise, it is very difficult for many people to admit that the things of our faith cannot ultimately be demonstrated.

Everything in Doubt Again

I'll begin with the question posed at the end of our last discussion. You gave us an idea about the historical accuracy of the four gospels, but your last statement left us very much in doubt again on this point. I looked up that text in the eighth chapter of John: "Before Abraham was, I am." The rest of the story, and in particular the end which says "Then they picked up stones to throw at him," reads as if the author were on the scene when it happened. This reminds me of another text. When Jesus stands before the High Council he is forced to bear witness to himself. He does it by stating explicitly that he is the Son of God. If all of this is no longer historically true, what is? Not too long ago I heard a priest say that the text "Before Abraham was, I am" is perhaps the most sublime recorded word that Christ ever spoke.

I could certainly agree with that opinion. But this does not mean I believe Jesus himself spoke those words exactly as written. That seems historically impossible. I shall try to explain this a little, even though it seems like a terrific trapeze act to explain these intricate problems in a few minutes time.

Allow me first to recall the development of the gospels. Let's take Matthew or Luke. These books are both divided into four parts or sections. First is the story of Jesus' birth and early youth. Then comes the longest part by far, the story of his public life, his preaching, miracles and journeys through Palestine. In the third part his capture, the court proceedings, his suffering, and his death are described. This part consists of only a few chapters; although it may seem short, relatively speaking it's an extensive account, since the events took place in a few days. Finally, the fourth section contains a series of stories about Jesus' apparitions after his death.

Through education and habit we used to read such a gospel as a biography. We imagined the evangelist as a biographer describing the facts from the beginning to the end, and without any further thought we took for granted that all the stories represented facts of identical order and validity. Since the beginning of our discussions you have become familiar with the notion that it is not as simple as that. Recall how differently factual events were handled in Samson and in the story of David and Uriah. In reading the gospels also we have to get used to a great variety of relationships between the stories and the actual events.

Preaching in Reverse

The New Testament itself gives us the necessary instructions for this. In the book of Acts we see what the apostles set out to do after Jesus appeared to them. In the second chapter, Peter speaks to the Jews of Jerusalem: *"Men of Israel, hear these words: Jesus of Nazareth, a man attested to you by God with mighty works and wonders and signs which God did through him in your midst, as you yourself know—this Jesus, delivered up according to the definite plan and foreknowledge of God, you crucified and killed by the hands of lawless men. But God raised him up . . . This Jesus God raised up, and of that we all are witnesses . . . God has made him both Lord and Christ . . . Repent and be baptized . . ."* (Acts 2, 22-38)

This and the following chapters of the Acts of the Apostles contain the fundamental outline of the first preaching. The starting point is the man "Jesus from Nazareth" who through his miracles and sermons gave evidence of being a great servant of Yahweh. The Jews had him executed but God rehabilitated him—put him in the right—by calling him back to life. In all of this, repeated reference is made to Old Testament texts. "This horrible death was not the miserable failure of a career which started out so promisingly (as we, his disciples, once thought). It was not a punishment by God for an unparalleled pride. No, Jesus submitted to the role that God had planned for his Messiah. This we can prove to you from the scriptures. Renounce the past and take part in the new and definitive situation which began with the resurrection of Jesus . . ." This is a condensed form of what we find in the second and third chapters of the Acts, in Peter's speeches in chapters four and five, in his words to Cornelius in chapter ten, and also in Paul's address in chapter thirteen.

The first thing to be announced was the resurrection of a man who had been executed a short time before, as each person in the audience knew. Soon a second element entered. For the benefit of those people who had not heard of the crucifixion, the apostles had to relate how it all happened, the arrest, the motives leading up to it, the trial, the role of Pilate and the story of Jesus' death. Before long, a third element followed. Those who listened to the call of the apostles and who accepted Christ as their Messiah and Lord, soon began to ask all sorts of questions. How did it happen that the true Messiah had been killed by the leaders of his own people? Had his teachings provoked this? What did he mean by the "kingdom of God," a term so heavily charged for every Jew? All these were questions about which the disciples were very much concerned and which kept them searching almost feverishly during that early period.

Finally, a few disciples started to meditate and think about Jesus' mysterious personality, and his unique relationship with God, whom he calls Father in such a special way. To them it was apparent that Jesus had received an abundant share of the fullness of life. The disciples could best reflect on Jesus when reading the scriptures of Israel. In these God had said much about his actions, his way of treating mankind, about the wisdom with which he created and with which he now governs the universe, about the mediators and the prophets he had sent to his people. They could read about the tasks that he had assigned to David and his successors as the "anointed of Yahweh" and about the promises he made.

With all of this as a help they meditated on Jesus' person. Sometimes they gave their views in the form of stories about the beginnings—about Jesus' birth and youth. These "theological" stories inspired Matthew and Luke when they wrote gospels. From the very beginning they tried to explain what Jesus intended to be for his faithful: the Messiah, the Son of God.

So much for Matthew and Luke. Mark's Gospel, which came first, did not include stories about Jesus' birth. However he, too, immediately characterized Jesus with a "theological" story referring to his beginnings. He described the opening of his public life, his baptism in the Jordan, but not his earlier beginning as a human being.

John goes further and deeper, delving into Jesus' personality. He goes back to the absolute beginning which lies in eternity. He describes the mystery of Jesus' person in the awesome prologue to his gospel about the Word that was with God and was God and in Jesus became "flesh"—that is, a concrete historical person.

The material of the gospel stories, therefore, first appeared in the reverse order to that which the gospels follow. Jesus' resurrection was the first thing the disciples preached about, but it's the last thing recorded in each of the gospels. The birth and early years of Jesus were not subjects of preaching until much later, but they are the first things recorded in the chronology of the gospels.

Jesus Pointed toward God Alone

If I remember correctly, Christ sent his disciples out to preach in Galilee before the resurrection. They were to announce that the Kingdom of God was near and that the people must be converted. But in the sermons after the resurrection which you just referred to, we hear no more about that Kingdom of God. It seems that the disciples did not obey their instructions.

The first part is true, and your observation brings us a step further. Jesus did speak to the Jews about God, or rather he introduced God's call and conveyed his demands. After the resurrection the apostles spoke to the Jews about Jesus as the Messiah who had come. A shifting of the central subject had taken place: Jesus' preaching about God became the disciples' preaching about Jesus.

In our earlier discussions we saw how resolutely Jesus defended the rights of God and man. More distinctly and more directly than all the prophets before him, he told the Israelites what God expected of them. He did this in such a manner that people were obliged to listen and to make decisions. They could no longer justify themselves by fulfilling certain commandments. God appealed to their hearts through the preaching of Jesus. All privileges whatever evaporated into nothingness. Through this human being shone the Holy One of Israel before whom all self-sufficiency is swept away (Is. 2, 12-17).

Jesus himself seemed to be the voice of God. He apparently did not want to weaken the effect of this by drawing attention to his own person. Someone addressed him once as "Good Teacher." This was meant as flattery, implying, "O excellent teacher, tell me . . ." He responded almost harshly: *"Why do you call me good? No one is good but God alone"* (Lk. 18, 18-19). He was almost a monomaniac, completely taken up with God. Mark tells us that he and his disciples were so wrapped up in the preaching of God's kingdom that they even neglected to eat. Christ's relatives were concerned and said, "It is time that we do something about this. Truly, *he is beside himself"* (Mk. 3, 21).

The disciples who were constantly with him often wondered

who he really was. An excellent teacher, yes, but a teacher of a very particular kind. He never quoted statements of other great rabbis. He was more like the prophets of old; however, he spoke much more directly. Even the greatest prophets began every proclamation with, "Thus speaks Yahweh, the God of Israel." Jesus never did this. He began simply, *"I say unto you."* Sometimes the stately and liturgical "amen" preceded his message: *"Amen, amen, I say unto you . . ."*

This authoritative teacher and leader was at the same time a cordial and attentive friend. It was good to be with him, to be in his service. But who he really was—this the disciples had to guess. Peter once put an end to the probing questions of some people saying, "I know who you are: *You are the Christ"; and he charged them to tell no one about him* (Mk. 8, 29-30). In the next chapter he gives them a similar command to keep silence. It is strange at first sight that those who are accepted by Jesus to announce the Kingdom of God may not say anything whatsoever about what they know of Jesus!

Yet this made sense. During the Roman occupation unrest was brewing in all areas. This was especially the case among the spirited Galileans. A person needed only to state with a little bravado that he was the Messiah and the smoldering fire of resistance would burst into flames. Pilate (the Roman governor) always kept troops on alert to smother a possible revolt, especially around the great feasts when so many Jews from all over the country came to Jerusalem. When the ordinary people, tired of the Roman occupation, heard the word "Messiah," they thought of a fighter, who (with the help of God naturally) would drive the Romans into the sea once and for all. That is why Jesus did not want to be called "Messiah." The title was too provocative. God had different plans for the authentic Messiah. John is certainly referring to a true historical memory when he tells that Jesus withdrew into solitude after the multiplication of the loaves because he saw, *"that they were about to come and take him by force to make him king"* (Jn. 6, 15). If you read the accounts of the Passion, you notice all sorts of details concerning that political suspicion. The priests, the Sadducees in particular, wanted above all a good relationship with the occupying power. They feared that Jesus' appearance in Jerusalem at the Passover might cause riots. That triumphal entry with palms waving and those messianic slogans was a dangerous affair; no less dangerous was Jesus' authoritative action against the merchants in the temple. In such riots the Roman soldiers would take action, and that could cause a national catastrophe. It was better to do away with this man quietly.

But didn't Christ tell his disciples what his end would be?

Yes, but probably not with all the minute details with which the evangelists recorded those predictions. At any rate, little or nothing of their meaning penetrated the disciples' way of thinking. You remember Peter's protest the first time that Jesus spoke about suffering, and how Jesus rejected this with the fiery words: *"Get behind me, Satan"* (Mt. 16, 23).

Do you mean Peter really acted like a tempter or seducer, like Satan?

Yes, for the usual concept of the Messiah being a particularly "successful" man, was forced upon Jesus from all sides. Naturally, this must have appealed to him much more than the road of humiliation and failure that the Father had mapped out for him. Quite naturally he was frightened by the latter. Therefore Peter's protest was a real temptation.

During the last months of his life he seems to have associated more with his intimate disciples than with the people. But in spite of these last instructions, Jesus' humiliating death was an unexpected turn of events for his disciples—the end of everything. They had built up such high hopes concerning the Messiah. Now the cold facts were manifested: he was not the Messiah.

Belated Recognition

On that first Easter day Jesus suddenly appeared in their midst and said, "I am indeed the Messiah of God." Although astonished and still a little perplexed they answered, "Yes, of course; now we know with whom we have associated all this time." It was a "belated recognition." Here's an example of what I mean. It's not quite what I want; you may find a better one yourself. In an exclusive lingerie store a housewife is standing next to a woman who is being helped by a salesgirl. She notices how exceptionally well groomed and well dressed the woman is. Her manner of speech is precise and clear. She leaves without paying and without saying anything about a bill. Our housewife continues to shop and forgets about the woman. Not until the next day when she reads in the paper that a visiting European queen, incognito, had done some shopping that afternoon does she realize, "Of course that was the queen! Now I understand everything." She had a certain mental image of the queen, but had not associated the behavior of the lady with this image. The connection was made suddenly when she read about it in the paper. Only then could she understand and relate her observations.

However unrealistic the comparison may be, it can help to illustrate the experience the disciples had. One element of it was the new insight into the scriptures that he gave them. Luke pictured this experience in an incomparably beautiful way in his story about the walk to Emmaus. The Lord him-

self showed his disciples how everything that had happened
to him had been indicated in the scriptures. He alone had recognized the will of his Father in those texts. Now, at this "belated recognition" he could share this knowledge with them
like an unexpected gift.

*So this is a definite fact, this resurrection of Christ. It's not
something you will later urge us to "see that a little differently"?*

No, this is *the* definite point on which all of the New Testament is founded, and the Church. It is precisely because the
resurrection of Christ is a different kind of resurrection from
the dead than for example the resurrection of the boy from
Naim or of Lazarus. They came back to normal life as a sort of
reprieve and had to die again; it was a stay of execution, so to
speak. Jesus came back in a new kind of human existence which could no longer be touched by death, as St. Paul
explicitly states. This created for Jesus the possibility of being
with his disciples in a new way. Restrictions of place and time
no longer existed for him.

As we saw before, the whole purpose of his actions and
preaching was to bring God to the people, to let them meet
God. This was the reason for his being. After he had made
the supreme self-sacrifice by dying, he received a new capacity
to be the living meeting place between God and man forever.

This is how the faithful through the ages understood the
meaning of the resurrection. We know that Jesus is actively
present among us in all kinds of ways. He is present where two
or three are gathered together in his name, in particular at the
celebration of the eucharist, the holy mass. The "technical"
manner as to how he is present in the Mass we leave to
theologians. Every Christian knows that he participates

in Christ's supreme act of self-sacrifice in order that he too may grow in that giving of self which is necessary to be able to love.

The Freedom of the Evangelists

I think we are getting away from our topic. I'd like to have an answer to my first question.

We really didn't change the topic. The method of the evangelists is founded on the belief that the risen Christ is in the midst of his disciples. Exactly because of that faith, no objections were made when Jesus was described as saying things during his public life which he really could have said only after his resurrection.

You should read sometime the seven letters with which the book of Revelation (or the Apocalypse) begins. These letters to the Churches were written by an apostle. Just as the prophets of Israel addressed their people as representatives of Yahweh, "Thus speaks the Lord . . ." this author writes representing Christ: "The words of the Son of God . . . I know your works . . . But I have this against you . . . that you do certain things wrong . . . To him who does my will, shall I give eternal life . . ."

The person who is talking must have a strong faith.

I should prefer to say that he must be someone who had received a leading role, or clearly a prophetic role, in the Church either from Christ or from an apostle. At any rate he was a person who knew he was speaking for the Lord of the Church, and in his behalf.

If you keep this in mind you will not be shocked by the

"discrepancies" we discover when we analyze the gospels historically. For example in the fourth chapter of Mark we find the parable of the sower. Afterwards Jesus explains its meaning. All exegetes agree that this explanation was not given by Jesus but by an early Christian preacher. The evangelist simply puts these words in the mouth of Christ. I could give you a number of such examples.

The fourth evangelist meditated more about the mystery of Jesus' person than did the others. We saw that Jesus put his own authority above that of Moses, thus attributing divine authority to himself. He also justified his own attitude toward sinners by referring to God's attitude. The "belated recognition" made it clear why he could do all this: he came forth from God's own essence; he was the Son of God, the eternal Word. Paul quotes from an old hymn which says, *"God has given him a name which is above all others,"* namely, divinity. John lets Jesus himself put this into words. When talking about Abraham, Jesus states that he is greater: *"Before Abraham was, I am."* At the same time this is a reference to that name above all others, "Yahweh," in which the Jews heard the meaning: "He is."

But how did I get the impression that the evangelist was there in person when Jesus said this?

Because the evangelist was such an excellent writer. However he didn't let himself get carried away with his imagination. The grand statement of Christ expressed truly what his historical actions and words implied. There is also the gesture of the people picking up stones to kill him. The enemies of Jesus had already plotted to kill him (already in Mark 3, 6), and this plan was finally carried out. Again John shows his talent for writing in the vivid and violent discussions which Jesus had with the Jews. It is historically accurate that Jesus was often in debate with the Pharisees and lawyers. As reported by John these dialogues also reflect later discussions between Jews and Christians. The latter separated from the Jewish community slowly, in a difficult and painful process. They gradually came to understand that they had to form a separate group, and that this separation was a necessary consequence of their belief in Jesus.

I have to admit that it will take some effort to get accustomed to the nature of the Gospels which you propose.

Yes, this is to be expected. We have been educated in the certainty that the bible is true. Automatically we thought that we could respect this truth only by accepting those stories as documentaries, with the accuracy of photography or tape recordings. We were looking at it very scientifically, forgetting its human elements.

It is, for example, very human to tell a story about a historical person by letting him speak in the first person. Imagine that Napoleon intended to capture all of Europe and then to become emperor. I might write that Napoleon said to his troops: "I want to conquer all of Europe and to become the emperor." Only a very narrow-minded pseudo-scientist would reproach me by saying, "I checked all the sources and there is not one document to give evidence of such a statement by Napoleon." Every normal person would accept my description. Such a summary of someone's intentions in the first person is quite human. Moreover, the evangelists were living in the Israelitic-Jewish tradition. In this tradition story telling had been in use for centuries, for a deeper reason. This is especially true in the case of Moses. He served as mediator between God and the people when the covenant was made. Through the centuries its conditions were proclaimed each year in the liturgy.

Those who did this in the ceremony fulfilled Moses' role. When circumstances changed and new rules had to be added, the authors let the story read that God handed these rules to Moses. The beautiful speeches in the first eleven chapters of Deuteronomy were written in the seventh century B.C. You may recall the statement, *"You shall love the Lord your God with all your heart, and with all your soul . . ."* (Deut. 6, 5) It is simply stated that Moses spoke those encouraging words shortly before his death, as a "farewell speech." In the same manner, an apostle could explain to the faithful what Jesus wanted to say to them in their own circumstances by putting the words into the mouth of Jesus himself.

As far as our faith is concerned, it doesn't make any difference whether or not Jesus himself spoke in the gospels. What matters is the inspiration which he gave by his presence, and it was John's purpose to present this to the people.

Exactly!

But how do you explain the other statement which I quoted in an earlier question, namely Jesus' words to the High Court: "You have said so"?

As related by Matthew and Luke, I should say it is an evading answer. In other words it does not mean "yes"; it means: "You said it and that is your responsibility." As far as I can see, this agrees with his whole attitude. He leaves the people in the dark about his person. This is also the reason why he steadfastly refuses to perform a miracle for people who demand it as proof that he is truly sent by God. They never get him to do it. For Jesus can only be accepted by faith.

No Proof of God

So to believe means to renounce one's intelligence?

No, but it does mean to give up your self-conceit, your urge to let everything center around and be subservient to yourself. Neither proof nor argument is strong enough to accomplish this. Your egotism always finds a counter-argument. In faith we are concerned about a subject of a different order, the order of personal relationships. God exists only for him who allows him to exist.

But with this you move everything into the area of subjectivity.

Yes. As a reaction to the earlier approach we must at present stress subjectivism; I have to admit it. We are reacting against a way of believing which we now consider as wretched degeneration. The theology of the last centuries and the doctrine of faith which was presented to us led us to believe that man could prove everything: the existence of God, revelation, the divinity of Jesus Christ, the true Church, and so on. The miracles served as proofs. In this manner God was lowered to the order of things of nature existing independently and impersonally. God seemed to be the great "clock-maker" who every now and then intervened to prove that he is still there. But the God of the bible does not exist in the same manner as, for example, do the Van Allen belts around the earth. The existence of these belts can be proved. God does not belong to this order. If you look at it this way, God does not exist.

Can nothing of our faith then be proved? Must everything remain a purely subjective, personal matter?

Yes, but if there is a group of people who have the same subjective conviction, as in our case, and all of whom have accepted the same attitude concerning life, then I would say that this conviction has become somewhat objective and rises above the individual. The requirement that all live in accordance with their convictions demands that those "unprovable convictions" be formulated in words. When the group is large, the cast on the world's stage changes regularly. Old people go, young people come. What remains are the formulas, the expressions, and the concepts.

It is noteworthy that our last discussion on the bible ended with this thought. The bible is in fact a reflection of the subjective convictions which Israel upheld, which Jesus lived completely, to which he drew his disciples and out of which the Church lives.

Then there is no real connection between the faith of the Church—that subjective faith—and the objective sciences of nature, for example?

No, the only existing connection is with the man himself who is engaged in these sciences. True researchers never cease to be astonished. They constantly discover new data whose secret laws they are probing. Such a researcher can say, "Man has certainly developed magnificently!" He can also say, "God, how magnificently you have put all of this together!" Yet this is a matter of personal attitude. A scientist will never bring this into a scientific discussion with colleagues. However, it will fill his song of praise when he is singing with other members of the Church—a song of praise about God who is so great that he can be modest and not have to force himself upon man. As a theologian recently stated, "It is not God's nature to demand a place of his own in this world."

ELEVEN:
The Paradise Story

In discussing the bible, many persons ask about the biblical account of the creation of the world and of man. From the terminology the basic question really is this: "Since the biblical account of the origin of the world and of man differs so greatly from the description given by modern science, what are we to think of the truth of the bible?"

In our discussions we purposely did not begin with the first chapters of the bible about the creation of Adam and Eve. Israel had already lived in contact with its God for some centuries when these chapters appeared. A great deal had been said and written about people, their mutual relations and their relation to God. This was done in the form of stories, commandments, proverbs, sermons, and meditations; eventually these famous chapters about the creation of the world and the sin of the first human couple were written—well-wrought pieces of art which had been in the making for centuries. Therefore, a person will understand them better and enjoy them more as he acquires greater knowledge of the rest of the bible. Now I'll discuss the first part of Genesis, but with two restrictions: I shall limit myself to the paradise story (Gen. 2 and 3) and I shall make only a few introductory observations about it.

Tribes Pictured as Individual Persons

This may seem to be a long preface to the question, but like an athlete trying for a broad jump we will need a long running start. We shall discuss two ways of thinking and of portraying things which apparently go back as far as Israel's beginning. The first one is the following: As it appears from old stories in Genesis, it was customary in those early tales to describe a group of people as an individual person and the relationships between different groups as family relationships.

To understand this more clearly, try to picture the Near East with Palestine in the center. That's where Israel lived. When it grew into a great kingdom during the time of David, it came into contact with other countries through commerce, and so on. Israel divided these peoples into three groups. The one in the east in and around Mesopotamia was called *Shem*. The Assyrians, for example, belonged to that group and were called "sons of Shem." Further away, but still belonging to that group, was the country of Elam with its inhabitants, the Elamites. Thus Shem also had a "son" named Elam. Where we would say, "These two belong to the same group," in Israel they said, "They are 'sons' of the group taken as a whole."

The people in the northwest and west, in Asia Minor and on the Greek Islands, including Cyprus and Crete, were called *Japheth*, and the smaller groups were again referred to in like manner. One of its "sons" was named Jawan or Joen— the Ionians of our history books. They lived along the eastern coastline of the Mediterranean.

The group southwest of Israel was named *Ham*, and its divisions were also called "sons." Egypt, the real Egypt of the Nile for example, was called a "son" of Ham, and so was Ethiopia. The coastal region was formerly known as Canaan. This name meant "purple snail." The whole coastal area was characterized by snails which washed ashore in great numbers and which had been used to make purple dye as long as people could remember. So it became "purple country." In Greek "purple" was called "phoinix" and the country, *Phoinikia,* is our Phoenicia.

To whom did this purple country belong? The Israelites knew that it had been under Egyptian influence culturally and politically. Practically speaking it was a part of Egypt. Therefore they said, "Canaan is a son of Ham" or "Ham is the father of Canaan." Of course Canaan was divided into smaller parts, one of which was the city Sidon, the oldest and most important city of that period. When I talk about Sidon I can't help but think of the sweater I am wearing. I bought it there two years ago. At that time I took part in the excavation of a cave which is between sixty and seventy thousand years old. This project was under the supervision of an English lady, Miss Garrod, one of the closest friends of the late Father Teilhard de Chardin. He was, as you recall, an "evolution scientist." When we weren't working and sat discussing evolution, I sometimes felt cold, and so I bought this sweater in Sidon. Although not as old as the cave, Sidon is a very old city. How did the Israelites express this? We would say, "Sidon was the oldest and most important city of Canaan," but the Israelites said, "Canaan became the father of Sidon his first-born" (Gen. 10, 15). What I have now roughly explained is truly the background of that whole chapter, the so-called list of nations. This manner of expression, therefore, did not mean that these were real fathers and sons; it meant that a given city was the most important part of a certain country.

This is one principle. If you continue to think along this line you will understand quite a number of other matters. In the country situated on both sides of the river Jordan lived at a certain time the people of Israel, consisting of twelve tribes. There was a tribe Naphtali named after the area of the same name. The members of that tribe were called the "sons of Naphtali." More to the south was the area called Ephraim, and still further south was the mountain area of Judah. All twelve tribes together then formed Israel. To express this one would say, "Israel has twelve sons."

This method of interpretation was excellent material for the fabrication of stories, in particular when memories of historical individuals, real patriarchs, were identified with the personification of groups.

When scripture spoke of Shem, Ham and Japheth, the only groups of people the early Israelites knew, one would expect the following: The three groups together might be humanity, or "adam." Thus, "Adam had three sons." Perhaps it was sometimes said this way in early Israel. But when the story of the flood was incorporated into the bible, this no longer made sense. Then it had to be Noah, the lone survivor, who begot Shem, Ham and Japheth.

Stories of Origin

Now we shall discuss the second ancient way of thinking. People liked to describe the situation or the characteristics of a certain group by telling the story of its origin, in which the meaning of the names often played an important part. I shall give two examples. In Edom, southwest of Israel on the mountain Seir, lived the Edomites. This tribe had been conquered by Israel during the reign of David. Edom existed and became a kingdom before Israel. It was also related to Israel, which now considered the Edomites as its subjects. This seemed to be an unacceptable situation, a relationship difficult to describe. An attempt is made by telling the story of Edom's origin which you can read in the twenty-fifth chapter of Genesis.

Rebecca carries twins in her womb. Esau, who represents Edom, is born first and then Israel (also called Jacob) follows. The name "Edom" may mean or have connection with the word "reddish," and Seir sounds almost like the word for "hairy." Jacob means "he deceives," derived from the phrase "to hold by the heel." So in the bible story it is related that the first-born, Esau, was reddish and hairy, and Jacob was born holding Esau by his heel. Such a story reports the "origin" of these groups of people while at the same time picturing in a factual situation the mutual relations of the two tribes.

The second example is an answer to a question mailed in to me. The person diligently began to read the bible, but when he reached the nineteenth chapter of Genesis, he writes, "I had to stop! This is going too far." In that chapter the two daughters of Lot who live alone with their father want to have children. They seduce their father while he is drunk and become pregnant by him. The person who wrote the letter continues, "This is downright incest, and with not a word of disapproval! In my opinion this cannot be the word of God."

What is this story really about? It tells us about Ammon and Moab, two tribes despised by the Jews, living east of Israel beyond the macabre, cursed Dead Sea. An Israelite heard a familiar word in each of these tribal names. In Ammon the word *amm* indicates a close relative, or even a father. In Moab the *ab* is the normal word for father. The 'm' can mean "from" or "out of." Thus it becomes clear what the story has to tell us. The Israelites knew that the tribes Ammon and Moab were related, and they did not have a high opinion of them. And so in the Genesis story of their origin, Lot, the cousin of Abraham, is described as having two daughters with whom he flees from Sodom. Each of them begets a child by her father and therefore one is called "son of my relative" or "Ammon" and the other "from father" or "Moab." The story is not meant to relate a fact that happened long ago, but to illustrate the situation of these tribes through a description of their origin.

The Author of the Paradise Story

When, in the book Genesis, certain groups of people are characterized by an "origin story," then a story about the origin of humanity as a whole, the "adam," would intend to characterize the situation and nature of humanity. In the ninth or eighth century B.C., an Israelite expressed in Genesis what he thought of "the phenomenon of man." In other words he described the situation and nature of "man" according to the ancient way of thinking, that is, by means of a story of his origin, allowing the meanings of certain words to fulfill a function. The writer must have been a great thinker and a great poet, and we shall never completely understand the depths of his story. To try to grasp the meaning we can set up a number of questions before starting to read. For example: What was the world of the author like and what were his convictions? From what standpoint did he judge? What struck him when he looked at human life from his viewpoint? Did he know any other stories of this kind or did he create the paradise story from his own imagination? What role was this paradise story to have in the entire historical work that he was writing?

The answer to the first question is easy to give and explains a great deal. The author was an Israelite, and thus his life was governed by the covenant. Rather, his life was governed by the deity with whom the people of Israel had a special relationship, so special that he was named "God of Israel." This was based on actual facts. God had saved Israel from the power of Pharaoh who wanted to destroy the nation. When they were without hope Yahweh rescued them and brought them into the Promised Land. There he gave them a choice. If they obeyed him as their divine Savior and only Lord, and if they remained loyal to each other, they could live peacefully in God's beautiful country and enjoy his blessing. If they revolted against him they would be driven from this land (Deut. 30, 15-20). At least once a year every Israelite heard those facts proclaimed and learned again how God let him choose for himself.

Here the structure of the paradise story is molded. Adam is created from nothingness. God leads him into the beautiful garden and gives him a commandment. This gives Adam the choice of staying in the garden and continuing to live happily there or of rebelling and being driven from the garden into death.

The Phenomenon of Man

As appears from this structure, the author saw the nature of man as determined by that very thing which Israel experienced so explicitly in the covenant relationship: God had given them life, and also the choice to accept or refuse this dependence on him. The first important question which he posed was: "What is it that urges us time and again to say 'no'? Why are even the best among us, such as David, sometimes driven, as it were, toward evil? We commit the evil ourselves, that is clear, and yet it seems as if we are spurred on by a force beyond us, and that force cannot be God!

"Further, we have a relationship with 'the living God' who possesses life in its fullness and wishes to share it. Why then do we have to die? And even here in his own country in which we live, fruit trees don't spring up everywhere from the soil; why do we have to toil so hard to wrangle something edible from among the thistles and thorns? And why do our women have to endure such difficulty and pain to bring children into the world? Giving birth should be something pleasant, an exuberant joy. Is this also related to a disturbance in our relationship with the living God?

"What about the animals? We humans have so much in common with them. Yet we are above them. We are partners of God. We can be disobedient. An animal cannot. But why can animals live so carefree without clothing? Why has man the need, the necessity to cover his nakedness before someone else? Is this also an indication of a possible disturbance? Is this perhaps the physical sign of a much deeper disturbance, the impotence of a human being to reveal his inner self completely? Is this the reason why in the final analysis everyone remains, deep down inside, a stranger to the other, even to his most dearly beloved?"

Astonishing also is the fact that man, "adam," does not really exist. What really exists is man and woman. In Hebrew the word "woman" appears to be the feminine form of the word "man." How tremendously different they are, "man" and "woman," and yet how irrepressibly they are drawn to each other. Each of them is an independent and responsible person. Yet only together, united, is the "adam" complete enough to bring forth another human being. Could this remarkable feature be best characterized by a story about their origin in which they are one in the beginning, one inside the other, and then separated by God?

Elements from Elsewhere

Meditations of this kind furnished the author with all kinds of material for his story. However not all of it. Better than any one of us he knew a number of stories about the origin of man and the world which then circulated in neighboring countries. In the last hundred years we've come to know more of them. In the story of the flood we saw an example of how Israel derived material for stories from other peoples. However we shall never find a story exactly like the bible story of paradise. This is because the Genesis story is in nature and structure too much determined by Israel's totally different way of living and thinking. At most the author may have borrowed a theme or suggestions for details from foreign works. In Mesopotamia a story existed about the origin of man. According to it, there was a revolution in the world of the gods. The rebel leader, Kingu, is killed; his blood is mixed with earth and from this man is formed. This seems to suggest that man is evil from origin. The bad was removed from the world of the gods and personified in the human body. Perhaps the biblical author reacted against this viewpoint by telling the story thus: "In the beginning God takes some dust from the ground (in Hebrew *adamà,* a play on the word "adam," man) and molds it into a human figure; then he breathes something of his life into it." Evil can in no way have its origin with God.

The motif of the "tree of life" had been used long before Israel existed. We already met with it in the epic of Gilgamesh, who secured the life-giving herb in the depths of the sea. When he refreshed himself in a pond on his way back to his city Uruk, this "life herb" was stolen by a snake. In the biblical story God makes "the tree of life." It is due to man's own free choice that he is deprived of it, not as the result of chance or some tragic fate.

In the paradise story a snake does appear. The words used to curse the snake were never so clear to me as on that summer day in 1947 when I met up with a snake in the heart of Palestine. I was assisting at the excavation of the biblical town of Tirzah, north of Sichem. One morning I walked to a hill in the neighborhood to take a bird's eye view photograph which would show how the place was situated. I was carrying a heavy plate camera, a specimen from about the turn of the century. On my way back I stopped for a moment to catch my breath. Something rustled behind me. A snake! It was ready to attack my heel. I threw all my gear on the ground, camera and heavy tripod, and I grabbed a stone to crush the snake's head, the only way to disarm one, but I missed. However the snake as a symbol in the paradise story will not escape this fate. On my way back to the excavation I thought up the story that I was going to tell in all its details, and I was certainly not going to forget to relate it to the Arabic workers. Then I realized that their word for snake is very similar to the word "life." Their language had preserved what the word "snake" meant for the people of the ancient Near East. That repulsive animal without legs, crawling out of the earth, seemingly genderless, which constantly rejuvenates itself was, for all sorts of reasons, a symbol of the deepest mysteries: life, fertility, secret knowledge. From excavations we now know something about the important role the snake played in the religion of the Canaanites. For the author of the paradise story the snake is "the most cunning of all animals," but at the same time "created by Yahweh." Separate from and independent of God nothing exists. It is the snake which seduces man (the feminine form of "adam" serves as point of attack) to eat the fruit of the mysterious "tree of knowledge." Thus the author tries to symbolize the strange urge in man to be one's own master, and the negation of one's deepest nature which man experiences in himself. At the same time man knows that these feelings cannot originate from God.

Curse and Blessing

Now just a word about the role which the author intended this story to play in his work as a whole. We have already spoken about the earliest version of Genesis. We also saw that Israel, probably in the era after David, began to be aware of its task involving all of mankind. Yahweh had entered into a special relationship with the Israelites in order to draw all other people into the covenant. This belief was illustrated in the story of Abraham's "calling." He was to become a "blessing" for all peoples (Gen. 12, 3). This is probably the reason why the second part of the paradise story is so overshadowed by the idea of "curse." In the stories immediately after it we see how this curse manifests itself more and more in the ever-spreading evil. Fratricide is followed by even greater perversion, and after the tower of Babel mankind is completely divided into groups that can no longer communicate with each other. All of this seems to serve as a dark background against which the "calling" of Abraham, personifying Israel, appears as a bright light.

These were only a few introductory remarks. I hope that it has at least become clear to you how not to read the story of paradise. It was not written with the intention of being an account of the actual historical beginning, but it was designed to characterize the situation in which man finds himself. Therefore, there can never be a contradiction between this story and the findings of modern science.

I've received a few letters which dealt with the problem of evil in this world. They came from people who struggle with this problem and who find it very hard to believe in a good God. The story of Genesis is an attempt to shed some light on this difficulty. The believing Israelite who wrote it was courageous enough to free God from every blame. However, in that eighth century before Christ the writer did not solve our fearful and frustrating problems. Neither did Christ bring a solution for all problems. However he did show us something in his life of the relationship between evil and God's infinite power. Nevertheless, the expression that God *permits* evil can be misunderstood to mean that he just calmly stands by. That is not so; yet he permits it in the sense that he has the power, considering the whole of creation, to bring good out of evil.

Father van Hemert writes in *School and Religion* for February 1965: "How he exercises that power is illustrated by Jesus: he does it by joining in the fight, even by perishing in it. Through his own pain he made suffering into redemption . . . However, this cannot answer all the questions of the human heart. But it points in the direction in which we see the solution come to life, namely in Christ. His life demonstrates how the truly infinite power of God is totally different, more mysterious, zealous, involved, and more redeeming in its fight against evil than we could ever imagine with our narrow human concepts of God's almighty power . . . Every question concerning God can be answered only in terms of God's appearing in Christ."

TWELVE:
Truth and Fiction

Certain biblical figures represent groups of people rather than individuals. This raises the question as to the criteria applied in making this statement. Biblical scholars carry on their historical research in the same manner as do their colleagues in "profane" history. This would seem a valid reason for using the historical sequence of events which the bible reflects in the teaching of secular history. And many parts of the bible should be included in courses which are designed to acquaint our young people with world literature.

Is Christ Fictitious?

Our discussions so far have caused me to wonder more and more about questions which have concerned me for some time. You showed how the actual history of people is identified with a fictitious person, a supposed progenitor. What is the actual criterion, the measuring rod, that is applied in judging whether something is history or fiction; whether some event happened or not? Could I say: "We are Christians whose history is founded on a fictitious person"? Do you know what I mean?

Yes, I believe so. It seems to me that your question contains two elements. From what I said about the stories of the origin of Canaan and Edom, you deduced some sort of principle of general validity, and now you ask if we may apply this rule to the Christians and to Christ as well. Secondly, you want to know more about the criteria which we apply in making such judgments about biblical stories. Let me answer one at a time.

You must have a rather philosophical mind to arrive at the question concerning Christ. A person continually engaged in the study of history soon learns that one cannot work with principles and prototypes, for no two facts or events are alike.

Between the two factors that you want to put into one category lies such an enormous distance, not only in time but also qualitatively, that we cannot really compare them. In one instance we're concerned with speculations about people whose past is completely unknown. In the second, we're dealing with a group of people united around an exceptionally inspiring historical person. I'll try to clarify this difference a little more.

You may recall that in the explanation of the "origin stories" I repeatedly spoke about "Israel's beginning" and about "the early Israelites" who characterized their neighbors with the aid of such stories. I also said that the ingenious author of the paradise story, who wrote in the eighth century or thereabouts, used this ancient way of thinking.

I explained these things without stressing them. Now I have to come back to them. In those early days Israel had a great deal of communication with all its neighbors, Ammon, Moab and Edom. However, the Israelites knew nothing about their past. At most they had a few vague memories of a migration of nations in which those other tribes had taken part. It could hardly be otherwise. To have definite knowledge about the past one must possess written documents. Only when a people reaches a certain stage of development and organization can the conditions necessary for recorded history be present. Israel did not reach this stage until the time of David. He was the man who transformed a farming community into an organized kingdom. We know that he borrowed talents from Egypt, where he also sent Judeans to be trained as government officials. The art of organizing thousands of people into a good functioning society had been known for some twenty centuries there. In this way David created the conditions in Israel which were necessary for writing literature. Under Solomon and in the century following, the literature of Israel was already enjoying its first era of grandeur.

Israel had some knowledge of its own past, the greater part of which had been passed on orally. Part of this referred only to the history of certain tribes and was kept alive in sanctuaries of local importance. During the reigns of David and Solomon, interested parties collected these traditions and enlarged and arranged them in cycles of stories, thus creating larger entities which were true literary works. They had no knowledge of or interest in stories about their neighbors' past. That is why these authors could freely use a popular way of imagining things and a daring play on words, as we saw the last time, to characterize actual relations in their "origin stories."

After the time of David, nearly eight hundred to a thousand years must have passed before we come to the era of Christ and the Christians. During these centuries the cultural development of Israel and Judah continued. They came into closer contact with highly civilized peoples in other areas, and with their many-faceted literature. Think of the library that Ashurbanipal (in the seventh century B.C.) established in Nineveh; excavations at this site have revealed some 20,000 documents. This Assyrian king gathered all the old literature that he could lay his hands on, complete with the necessary dictionaries. It is known that the last king of Babylon,

Nabunaid or Nabonidus, a century later, had a consuming interest in archeology and in the preservation of monuments. At that time a remnant of Jerusalem's population was living in Babylon. Among them was Ezekiel. From the book in the bible named after him we can see how much this priest and prophet knew about Babylonian culture. In the next century we meet the great organizers of the Jewish community, Esdras (or Ezra) and Nehemiah. They were officials at the Persian court and were very highly educated persons. Afterwards came the Greco-Roman culture with its numerous geographers and historians whose studies were concerned with Palestine and the Jews. The historical scene was indeed basking in bright light at the time when Jesus appeared. You may recall from our previous discussions what an incomparable personality speaks in the authentic recorded words of Jesus. The people he came into contact with are known to us from history: the Pharisees, Herod Antiphas, Caiaphas, Pilate. The Church, "the Christian people," grew out of the circle of his disciples; people who chose to follow him and might say, for example, "We shall not retort when we are reviled, for Jesus did not do that . . ."

There is an immeasurable difference between the two elements which you combined in that one question. There is a difference in quality, too. In the one case, the early Israelites speculated about people whose historical origin they did not know. In the other, we have a growing group of followers of a man who lived in recorded history, who came into conflict with other people and who was crucified by those people. Inspired by him, countless persons began a new way of life completely dominated by his person.

Between these two very different things lies a history of many centuries which I have sketched repeatedly as the historical background against which we assigned appropriate places to the biblical figures and the scriptures.

*But is this historical background accurate? Are there any
sources besides the bible which help to prove this?*

Very few, at least for the first and, to a certain extent, the
most important centuries. I want to make this as clear to you
as I can.

About the year 1250 B.C. we put the very important event
of the exodus from Egypt. No trace of this event is found in
the otherwise-rich Egyptian historical documentation. Later we
have the period of a tribal federation in Palestine with its
Judges. After that came Saul, who tried to establish a kingdom. Next was the great king David, followed by the famous
Solomon. Up to this time the only source for any of this is the
bible. This also holds true for the two separated states, Israel
and Judah, during the reigns of their first kings, whose names
and the years that they reigned were precisely recorded in the
bible.

I believe that the mention of King Ahab of Israel by the
Assyrian prince Shalmaneser III in his account of a battle
fought in 853 B.C. was the first non-biblical reference to
Israel. The memorial in stone of Pharaoh Mernefta (or
Merenptah), from approximately 1230 B.C., on which a certain "Israel" in Palestine is mentioned, is too uncertain to be
counted. Later military records of the Assyrian kings provided
some more information concerning Israel and Judah, along
with the many other small countries that were conquered.
About 701 B.C. Jerusalem was besieged. Besides the bible account of this we can also read the Assyrian one. In recent years
more documentation on the period which ended with the Babylonian destruction of Jerusalem has come to light. We are less
fortunate regarding the period which followed, when the
Israelites returned from Babylon and started to build the Jewish society. Finally, for the time of the Maccabees and there-
after extensive non-biblical records are available.

So this uncertainty pertains only to those centuries that preceded the era of the Assyrians?

No, you can't draw that conclusion. For those centuries we have to rely on Israel's own documentation. But why should that be less reliable?

Reliable Information

Precisely because faith plays such an important role in the works of the biblical authors. Don't their writings convey purely subjective opinions? Other people don't share that faith, so isn't their information about the Jewish people and the early Christians more reliable than the biblical records?

I deny that other people would be more objective. Even the greatest historians of Greece and Rome were not objective. They too had their "faith." They were convinced, for example, of the divine mission of their people, of the justice of certain wars, of the integrity of their heroes. When a modern historian tries to reconstruct what actually took place in a given century of Roman history, for example, he avails himself of such great authors as Livy and Tacitus. However grateful to them, he uses their works critically. He analyzes the author's temperament, his education, his preferences and his ambitions. He tries to discover the sources of the writer's information. All of this he takes into consideration when he comes to determine what was really "history" in his work and what was not.

So he does work with certain criteria to determine historical accuracy?

Yes, and I believe that we bible people examine the historical documents in our field just as critically. The only difference is that we are concerned with *other* subjective factors. Our classical colleague who studies Livy considers the Roman environment of his subject, along with the collective manifestations of faith that were prevalent then, and also such personal factors that may have influenced Livy in his description of the past. In the case of the biblical author, we are dealing with a Semitic culture with its own thought patterns and forms of expression. The author is not part of the Roman but of the Israelite tradition, and he derives his vision of man and of the world, as well as certain ways of presenting the past, from this tradition. He lives at a certain moment in Israel's development, and he witnesses certain historical trends.

In very old tales by anonymous story tellers from the time when there was no written literature, many of the components are difficult to define. Moreover, we have to consider the changes made by the generations who passed the stories on, and by the man who re-edited them for his written collection.

In studying the bible we use the same methods, and we apply —if you wish—the same criteria as do our colleagues of "profane" history.

That's news to me. I thought that this didn't apply to the bible. Sometimes it seemed as if you somehow decided on your own whether or not an event is historical.

I spoke purposely just now about "we" and "us" because someone reproached me for launching all sorts of personal opinions in these discussions. But, really, most of what I told you here is simply what normal biblical scholarship today is bringing into focus.

You had the impression that the bible was completely different from secular history. Perhaps this is because you aren't familiar enough with the normal work of a historian.

Non-technical books on history give only conclusions, and sometimes very hypothetical ones. They are based upon a patient examination of all sorts of documents which the reader never sees, and therefore never questions.

On the other hand we bible people are faced with the difficulty that every Tom, Dick and Harry has access to the documents from which we try to reconstruct the actual history of Israel, of Jesus and the early Church, for those documents are in the Bible. Since the average person does not know much about historical research, he is sometimes shocked by our conclusions. He thinks we are just inventing stories.

And then he asks for the criteria . . .

Indeed, it's easy to understand why one wants to know the criteria. We try our best to show some of our methods to people who are not of our profession, in particular to those who teach "bible history" or who use the bible in some way in their teaching. All who teach must keep up with the developments of science in their field. Why should we then make an exception for the bible?

Ways of Presentation

I sometimes try to summarize the peculiarities of historical writing as found in the bible under three headings. I sketch a simplified picture of the main ways in which the biblical presentations differ from those with which we are more familiar. Perhaps we shall find some material for an answer to your question about "criteria."

First, biblical writers are inclined to tie in certain customs and views of later periods with a definite historical starting point. Therefore the descriptions of certain "pioneering figures" and historical "turning points" are often overcharged with experiences and views of a later time.

The case of circumcision is very clear. This was customarily practiced by the ancient Egyptians and by tribes that bordered on Israel, except for the Philistines who were from a totally different cultural area. In Israel the practice of circumcision had, of course, some primitive and religious meaning, just as it had in the other countries. Circumcision, then, was not something peculiar to Israel until a remnant of Judeans arrived in Babylon as exiles. Since this rite was not customary in the Babylonian society, it quite naturally became something special —a sign that a person belonged to the Judean group. From then on circumcision became a "sign of the covenant." The covenant had, in the meantime, also been associated with Abraham, and that is how the story in the seventeenth chapter of Genesis came about.

In a similar way the liturgy of the temple at Jerusalem, and also the expansion of the liturgical regulations after the exile, were brought into conformity with the laws that Moses gave, or rather which he received from God after the sealing of the covenant at Mount Sinai. All the chapters in Exodus and Leviticus that list "liturgical" laws reflect for the greater part customs that came into use at a much later date.

A second peculiarity is much more obvious. The belief that God is behind all events leads to the tendency to make his activity visible by strengthening the miraculous element in the stories. In the earliest version about the escape from Egypt, it was a strong east wind which dried up an inlet of the sea right on time. In later texts the waters separate and the Israelites walk between two walls of water. In the book of Wisdom there is no longer any water in sight.

The number of quails, those edible birds which God dropped

in the desert to feed his people, is described somewhere as being so great that they were piled up three feet high in the desert and as far as a day's march around the camp of the Israelites.

Chapter twenty-four of the second book of Samuel describes how during an epidemic of the plague David offered a sacrifice, whereupon God let the plague disappear from the country. A few centuries later a Levite adapted that story for the book of Chronicles. He writes that David offered the sacrifice and that a fire descended from heaven consuming the sacrifice (1 Chron. 21, 26). He added this miracle to make God's intervention more clearly visible.

A third peculiarity is that, in the bible, a story which we could call factual in the modern sense may be set down among all sorts of unrelated stories. The transition from documented fact to a purely didactic story is made without any warning, such as: "Mind you, now I am suddenly switching from an old documented eyewitness story to a tale that was recently invented to illustrate some point."

Do I understand correctly from previous discussions that you believe these same peculiarities are also present in the New Testament stories, particularly in the gospels?

Yes, it would be strange if this were not the case. The people who passed on the memories of Jesus' words and deeds, and those who wrote the gospels, did not know any other way to describe the past than that of their Israelite-Jewish tradition. When we study the stories about Jesus' birth and youth, we should keep in mind their tendency to move certain insights ahead to the beginning. The same is true, though in a slightly different manner, when we read the story of Jesus' baptism in the Jordan, the beginning of his public life.

When the gospels furnish enough material to follow the development of a story, then we notice the second peculiarity as well: the growth of the miraculous element. Finally, the evangelists put stories one after the other without warning. In our critical opinion these stories differ greatly as far as their "historicity" is concerned.

You will understand that my description of these three "characteristics" of historical writing in the bible has been simplified. In reality, there is an immense variation which is of necessity curtailed by classification, and the relationships in each story are different.

The Bible in Teaching

Should a person who can think only in terms of clear "black and white" outlines concern himself with these questions?

No, but we are continually trying to reduce the number of such people. A great number of changes still have to be made in the method of teaching the bible. There seems to be a certain taboo connected with this book. Why shouldn't the real history of the people of Israel and the Jewish society, in as far as we can reconstruct it with the normal means of research, have a place next to the history of Egypt, Greece and Rome? Their histories have been reconstructed in exactly the same way.

Israel's historical documentation even appears to be a source for the history of other nations. Some time ago I wrote an article about Moab for the *Encyclopedia Britannica*. On that occasion I had to reexamine the facts. The world powers, Assyria and Babylon, swept the Moabites and all the small tribes in and around Palestine from the scene of history. They disappeared leaving hardly any traces. We find the name of Moab mentioned only a few times among the names of kings in the annals of the big powers. Accidentally—indeed quite accidentally—a stone with an inscription by King Mesja from about the year 840 B.C. has been found. Further historical data on the Moabites is preserved only in the bible, because when all the other small nations were destroyed forever, a handful of deported Judeans maintained their identity as a group in Babylon. This they managed to do on the strength of their conviction, their faith. They considered their God as a person, not tied down to a temple or a country, more powerful than any other force in history. On the strength of their religion this people remained in existence, maintaining its historical traditions and records. Because of these records we also know something about Moab.

Why shouldn't we be allowed to declare in history classes that we know more about the past of Israel than of all the other nations in its neighborhood, and that we have this knowledge today because of the peculiar faith of the Israelites. Their religion is no more difficult to describe, taken objectively, then the mythology of the Greeks and the opinions of their philosophers.

Jesus could also be discussed as one of the great figures of antiquity. Why not?

There was a time when people thought Jesus never existed.

Yes, but that time has gone. It is now clear to everybody that this thesis was based more on philosophical ideas than on a critical examination of the historical data.

Isn't the information about Christ one-sided, coming only from people who admired and adored him?

True, almost all information about Jesus comes from contemporaries who belonged to the circle of his disciples. But the question is, does that necessarily lead to falsification of reality? Every high school student learns about Socrates, his life and his philosophy. This man never wrote anything; practically everything we know about him comes from Plato, his disciple, his friend and admirer. The world accepts the judgment of this one man who is rightly famous for the depth of his thought and his philosophical imagination. Why should this information of a single person be more objective and more accurate than the information given by the group of ordinary people who surrounded Jesus? However, the taboo is there, and it will be hard to dispel.

I should also like to see the bible used more in the teaching of literature. Our high school students are exposed to a great number of writers from ancient to modern times, from all countries of the western world. The highly gifted court biographer of David, about whom we spoke, would cut a good figure among the greatest authors of our civilization. The same goes for the author of Job, and for so many lesser artists—such as the story tellers who participated in creating Genesis, the books Samuel, and the stories about Elijah and Elisha. The book of Jonah belongs to the category of the short story, as do a few parables of Jesus. Great connoisseurs of Greek literature consider Paul to be among the best authors of his century.

Fortunately, we have more freedom in the field of religious instruction. I think biblical anthologies should be made available in the higher grades of secondary schools. The anthologies should also be attractive enough for adults. Such books could present certain sections of the bible, none more than a few chapters long. Before each section there should be an interesting introduction, such as: "the author of the following selection was in this situation; he wanted to give this or that information; he used these figures of speech; and for us Christians of this time he has this or that message to proclaim."

Our time is up. May I conclude with the wish that such effective teaching aids will soon become available, giving more and more people the chance to acquaint themselves with the bible.